EXPERIENCING SCIENCE

Thinking Skills and Language Lessons for the Young Child

by Merle B. Karnes, Ed.D.

Illustrations drawn under contract by Cathie Lowmiller

Communication Skill Builders ®

3830 E. Bellevue/P.O. Box 42050
Tucson, Arizona 85733
(602) 323-7500

Duplicating

You may prefer to copy the designated reproducible materials by using stencils or spirit masters. It is not necessary to remove pages from this book. Make a single photocopy of the desired page. Use that photocopy to make a stencil or spirit master on a thermal copier.

© 1990 by

**Communication
Skill Builders, Inc.**
3830 E. Bellevue/P.O. Box 42050
Tucson, Arizona 85733
(602) 323-7500

ISBN 0-88450-468-9   Catalog No. 7689

10 9 8 7 6 5 4 3 2
Printed in the United States of America

For information about our audio and/or video products, write us at: Communication Skill Builders, P.O. Box 42050, Tucson, AZ 85733

About the Author

Merle B. Karnes, Ed.D., is Professor of Education at the University of Illinois, Urbana-Champaign. Dr. Karnes has a long history in the field of early childhood as a teacher, supervisor, administrator, researcher, and teacher trainer. She is a pioneer in the field of early education of handicapped children; and she is an expert in early identification and appropriate programming for gifted children, especially young gifted children. She is a prolific writer. Dr. Karnes's educational models for young handicapped children and for young gifted children are being replicated nationwide.

Her contribution to the field of education has been recognized over the years through honorary doctorate degrees conferred by a number of institutions of higher learning. She has also received numerous special awards from professional organizations. For example, in 1983 the University of Illinois Mothers Association presented her with a Medallion of Honor Award in recognition of her outstanding career in research and public service in the education of young handicapped children. In 1988, in recognition of her service to young exceptional children and to the Early Childhood Division of the Council for Exceptional Children, an annual award was established in her name. In this same year, a special award by the Illinois Planning Commission for Gifted Education was presented to her for her dedication and service to gifted/talented education.

Dr. Karnes is especially well known for the instructional materials she has developed. She is committed to working with children during the formative years so they will develop the attitudes, habits, skills, and knowledge that will build a strong foundation for future learning. Thus they may develop their potentials to the fullest.

Contents

Unit IV   Sound

Unit V   Light

Unit VI   Living and Nonliving Things

Unit VII   Plants and Plant Growth

Unit XII Magnetism

Acknowledgments

I wish to acknowledge the many creative ideas shared with me over the years by staff, university students, children with whom I have worked, and their parents. Those ideas have contributed to the development of *Experiencing Science: Thinking Skills and Language Lessons for the Young Child.*

The science curriculum is the culmination of more than twenty years of work. It has been fieldtested in various parts of the country with children representing a range of abilities, ethnic groups, cultures, and socioeconomic levels. The children ranged from three to eight years of age. Some were handicapped, some nonhandicapped, and others were gifted. To all teachers who used the curriculum and gave valuable feedback that led to revisions, a special thanks.

In particular I wish to acknowledge the contribution of Trenna Aukerman, whose assistance in the early development of this curriculum was invaluable. In recent years Paula Strong has had a major role in assisting me in revising activities and writing new activities. I am deeply grateful for her dedication in making this curriculum a valuable instructional resource for teachers and others who work with young children. We are proud to be able to share a product that both children and the teachers working with them will enjoy. We feel certain that children who are provided with this program will gain new insights and a better understanding of the science concepts included in this program.

Language-Based Lesson Plans for Science

The 109 language-based lesson plans detailed in *Experiencing Science* offer children a variety of projects in twelve areas generally considered to be part of science in the elementary school classroom. A major goal of these lesson plans is to help preschool children become increasingly aware of their environment in relation to themselves. Those areas that comprise their environment—air, water, sound, light, animals, weather, plants—are included. It is hoped that the children will acquire essential skills of observation and a vocabulary that will assist them in making further observations, asking questions, and expanding their knowledge of the environment.

Language Development—General Goals and Objectives

Goals

To improve processing and production of language
To improve categorization and classification skills
To increase and establish a basic vocabulary foundation
To improve ability to retrieve basic vocabulary
To increase ability to map meaning to vocabulary
To increase ability to combine and compare information in a meaningful manner
To increase the flexibility of language
To increase ability to make choices based on predictable outcomes
To develop effective communication skills
To improve auditory reception, association, and memory skills
To increase ability to analyze, sequence, and choose appropriately

Objectives

To identify pictures by name or by attribute
To compare similarities and differences of objects
To attend to directions
To sort items into categories
To respond appropriately to yes/no questions
To label objects
To complete phrases and sentences with appropriate vocabulary
To recall specific vocabulary in a given situation
To describe an object by its characteristics
To express a conclusion based on pertinent information
To use negatives in a simple sentence

Description of Science Units

A rationale and detailed explanation of the twelve science units and their recommended order of presentation follows. The final decision regarding what should be included and the order of presentation will depend on the individual teacher and the needs of the instructional group.

The *first unit,* "The Senses," is recommended as a beginning point because it deals with a subject with which the children already are familiar—their own bodies—and because the senses provide the channels through which subsequent knowledge is attained. In this unit the children learn to name their senses and to understand the abilities and limitations of each. They become aware of the interrelatedness of the senses, and they become cognizant of their dependence upon their senses in acquiring knowledge.

Following the increased awareness of their senses, the children proceed to use them to learn about the environment outside their own bodies. Air and water are substances that children experience every day; yet many children are unaware of the properties of either. In *Unit II,* "Air," the children learn that air is all around them, that air is in their bodies, that they breathe air, that air takes up space, that air can be moved, and that moving air has effects. In the *third unit,* "Water," they learn the uses of water, the forms of water and how these may be changed, and the meaning of *float* and *sink.*

Like water and air, sound and light affect us every day. In studying the *fourth unit,* "Sound," the children become aware of many sounds and of how they are produced and heard. They use their voices and ears under varying conditions. They become aware of the importance of vibrations in producing sounds and of the ability of vibrations to travel through substances such as air, wire, and wood. Several lessons deal with musical instruments and their classification into wind, string, and percussion types. The children acquire the vocabulary necessary to discuss sound-related ideas. The *fifth unit,* "Light," deals with natural and artificial light, the importance of eyes and light for seeing, the differences between day and night, the parts of the human eye, shadows, the colors contained in sunlight, and the results of mixing colors.

Unit VI, "Living and Nonliving Things," is a short unit designed to introduce the children to this important classification in general terms. They are taught simply that some things (plants, people, animals) are alive and some things are not alive. They become aware that they are alive, and they learn some characteristics of living things. The ideas introduced in this unit are broadened and used again in the units on plants, fruits and vegetables, and animals.

Unit VII, "Plants and Plant Growth," introduces the great variety of plants in the environment—trees, shrubs, flowers, grass. Lessons deal with plant parts (leaves, stems, fruits, flowers), plant needs (air, water, food, sunlight), and the planting and care of a bean and its growth sequence. Characteristics of trees are dealt with in more detail in the Weather and Seasons unit. Plants used for food are covered more extensively in the unit on fruits and vegetables.

In the *eighth unit,* "Fruits and Vegetables," the children's knowledge of plants is extended to include two types of plants that are eaten. They learn to identify some fruits (apple, banana, strawberry, pineapple, orange, lemon, grape, peach, pear, cherry) and some vegetables (potatoes, peas, lettuce, cabbage, corn, carrots, radishes, celery, cauliflower, broccoli). They become aware of the various forms of fruits and vegetables (raw, cooked, canned) and products made from them, such as juices. They participate in making common dishes (salad, vegetable soup, fruit cocktail) using fresh fruits and vegetables. In a game setting, they use the information they have learned to develop memory, association, and classification skills.

Unit IX, "Nutrition, Health, and Safety," leads the children from a consideration of fruits and vegetables as plants to a consideration of their value in helping to keep their bodies healthy. Lessons deal with the importance of eating a variety of foods, including fruits and vegetables; with the care and cleansing of the body; and with safety and traffic on the street. In short, attention is called to three aspects of care necessary for the children as living persons to stay healthy and alive. The teacher may expand each of these areas with additional lesson plans.

In *Unit X,* the children begin to study animals. In the first part, "Farm Animals," the children identify the cow, horse, pig, sheep, goat, and hen. They learn the body parts of each, the names of their babies, and the products they provide that are used by people. In the second part, the children study animals that are kept at the zoo. Although these animals do not constitute a part of the child's "real" environment, they are included because children see many zoo animals on television and read about them in books. The children are taught the names of the zebra, giraffe, elephant, camel, tiger, seal, walrus, porpoise, and dolphin. These animals are considered in two groups—those which generally move about by walking and those which generally move about by swimming—to give the child experience with subclassifications. Lessons deal with the imitation of animal movements and with similarities and differences among animals. Skills of sequential memory and classification are emphasized.

"Weather and Seasons," *Unit XI,* is intended for intermittent use throughout the year. Lessons 1 through 10 deal with the seasons and variations in everyday activities and in the physical characteristics of trees. Lessons 11 through 13 deal with weather—the wind, sun, snow, rain, and clouds. Activities and clothes associated with weather changes are discussed. Daily weather observation is recorded on a calendar. The unit provides activities that introduce and reinforce the concepts of seasons and weather in relation to time, and emphasis is given to firsthand experience with changes over time. It is imperative that these ideas be presented at seasonally appropriate times and discussed and reviewed frequently during the school year as changing conditions are observed by the children.

Unit XII, "Magnetism," may be considered supplementary rather than essential. In this unit, the children are introduced to some of the properties of magnets and the vocabulary to express them. An understanding of magnetism removes magnets from the realm of magic and helps the child realize that for every effect there is a cause.

Unit I
The Senses

Language Development— Goals, Objectives, and Vocabulary

Goals

To develop an understanding of the relationship between body parts and the five senses in perceiving the surrounding environment

To comprehend the significance of the five senses in recognizing and comparing the attributes and functions of objects in the surrounding environment

To utilize the five senses to identify and describe objects in the surrounding environment

Objectives

Receptive

The student will:

1. Identify body parts by name and by function

2. Comprehend the function of the sense of vision

3. Comprehend the sense of hearing and detect the directionality of a given sound

4. Comprehend the function of the sense of taste

5. Comprehend the function of the sense of touch and be able to discriminate items as rough or smooth, wet or dry, hard or soft, hot or cold, sharp or dull

6. Comprehend the sense of smell and be able to identify common smells

7. Associate the body part to the sense by name and by description

Expressive

The student will:

1. Describe body parts by characteristic and function

2. Use the sense of vision to describe an object with two or more characteristics

3. Name an object when given two or more visual characteristics

4. Label samples of food as tasting salty, sweet, or sour

5. Describe items as rough or smooth, wet or dry, hard or soft, hot or cold, sharp or dull

6. Identify common smells and describe other things that have a smell

7. Name each of the five senses

8. Use all five senses to describe a given item or object

Vocabulary

eyes	smelling	salty
ears	tasting	sour
nose	touching	rough
tongue	loud	smooth
hands	quiet	dull
senses	soft	sharp
seeing	hard	wet
hearing	sweet	dry

Lesson 1—*(Introductory)* Naming Body Parts

Objective—To identify eyes, ears, nose, tongue, and hands

Materials—

Picture of a child (see preparation instruction below)

Hand mirrors—one for each child (or a large mirror for several children to look into at once)

Crayons—five colors for each child

Preparing the materials—

Reproduce the picture of a child (page 15). Make a copy for each child in the group.

Procedure—

1. "Today we're going to talk about our senses. Our senses have to do with our eyes" (touch the appropriate part of your body as you speak), "our noses, our hands and skin, our ears, and our tongue. We use our senses to learn things about ourselves, others, and the world we live in."

2. Give children hand mirrors or tell them to stand in front of a large mirror. Have them look at their own ears, eyes, noses, tongues, and hands. Instruct the children:

   a. "Touch your ears."
   b. "Touch your nose."
   c. "Touch your tongue."
   d. "Touch your hands."
   e. "Touch your eyes."

3. Let each child select a partner. Ask one member of the pair to point to, in turn, the partner's ears, nose, tongue, hands, and eyes. Repeat, so the other member of the pair will have a turn to do the same.

4. Give each child a copy of the picture of a child and crayons. Give assistance as needed.

   a. "With your green crayon, mark the ears in the picture."
   b. "With your red crayon, mark the nose in the picture."
   c. "With your yellow crayon, mark the tongue in the picture."
   d. "With your orange crayon, mark the hands in the picture."
   e. "With your blue crayon, mark the eyes in the picture."

Lesson 2—*(Introductory)* Seeing

Objective—To name at least two characteristics of an object

Materials—Red ball

Procedure—

1. "We said we use our eyes to see. What are some of the things we can see with our eyes?" Let the children consider this question, and discuss their answers.

2. "Everyone, close your eyes. Don't peek! Keep your eyes closed until I tell you to open them. I am holding something." Hold up the red ball. "With your eyes closed, can you tell me what I'm holding? Can you tell me what color it is? Why not? Now open your eyes. What am I holding? What color is it? How do you know?" Conclude. "Yes, you can see it because you have eyes and your eyes are open. There are lots of things we learn by using our eyes. We learn about colors and shapes and many other things."

3. "Use your eyes and look around the room. When you see something, raise your hand and we'll ask you to tell us about it. We need to take turns so we'll be able to hear everyone." Encourage detail in description. If a child merely labels an object, help the child to tell more about it. "Tell us everything about it you can see." If necessary, ask questions: "What color is it? Is it big or little? What do we do with it? What is it made from?" Be sure each child has at least two turns to describe something.

4. "Now we're ready to play a game called I See Something. It's like the game we just played, but this time we won't name what we see; we'll just tell lots of things about it. We could tell what color it is, what you can do with it, how big it is—but we won't tell its name. While one of you

tells us about something you see, the rest of us will try to guess what you are looking at. I'll go first. Listen carefully, and look around the room. Try to guess what I am telling you about. Ready? I see something that is black. It's on the wall. You can write on it. It's bigger than the table." Continue to give clues until the children can guess the answer *(chalkboard)*. Give each child one turn to describe an object. Remind the children not to *name* the object but to tell about it.

Lesson 3—*(Introductory)* Hearing

Objective—When blindfolded, to point to the direction from which a sound is coming

Materials—Blindfolds—one for each child

Procedure—

1. "We use our eyes to see. We use our ears to *(hear)*. What are some things we hear with our ears?" Give the children time to think about this question and to supply a number of answers. *(We use our ears to hear people talking, to hear sirens, to hear dogs barking, to hear music, . . .)*

2. "Do you think you can hear if you close your eyes? Let's try. Everyone, close your eyes. Can you hear me? Why? Yes, we don't use our eyes to hear. Do you think you can hear if you cover your ears? Let's try. Put your hands over your ears." Gently tap the table. Then have the children uncover their ears. "Could you hear me tap the table when you had your ears covered? Why not?" If children were able to hear the taps, point out that they can hear *better* with their ears uncovered.

3. Seat children in a row on chairs or on the floor. "I'm going to blindfold you so you won't be able to see where I am. Then I'm going to walk in different parts of the room and say, 'Where am I?' When you hear me, point to where you think I am." Demonstrate a few times before blindfolding the children to be sure they understand the directions.

4. Blindfold the children. Walk to a point directly in front of them but at a distance of six or seven feet. Ask, "Where am I?" Remind the children to point to where the sound is coming from. Tell the children to keep pointing with one hand and to pull the blindfold off with the other hand. Have the children check to see if they were pointing correctly. Replace the blindfolds and play the game several more times.

5. Conclude. "We hear sounds with our ears. We also hear where sounds are coming from. We can tell if the sounds are inside the room or outside the room, in front of us or in back of us or beside us."

Lesson 4—*(Introductory)* Tasting

Objective—To identify foods as tasting salty, sweet, or sour

Materials—

Dish of sugar	Pretzels
Dish of salt	Gumdrops
Solution of salt water	Cake icing
Solution of sugar water	Napkins
Solution of vinegar water	Paper cups
Lemon slices	Pitcher of water
Concentrated lemon juice	Toothpicks
Potato chips	Blindfold

Procedure—

1. Place the dishes of salt and sugar on the table. "One of these dishes has salt in it; the other one has sugar in it. What would be the best way to find out which one is sugar and which one is salt? Can we tell them by looking? Can we tell by listening? No, we need to taste them to be sure. What part of our bodies would we use to taste them?"

2. Put a very little salt on each child's tongue by placing some on a toothpick, then touching the toothpick to the child's tongue. Use a clean toothpick for each child. "Is that sugar or salt?

How does it taste? Yes, salt tastes salty." Repeat for sugar, and label the taste "sweet."

3. Have the children taste the food items in the following order: the lemon, the three solutions, the gumdrops, the potato chips, the lemon juice, the pretzels, and the icing. For all items except the three solutions, ask the children to close their eyes. Remind them that they don't need their eyes to taste.

   a. Give each child a small taste of the item.
   b. Ask the child to name the item ("pretzel").
   c. Ask the child to identify the taste of the item ("salty").

   d. Restate the conclusion ("Pretzels taste salty").
   e. Have each child take a sip of plain water before tasting the next item.

4. Blindfold each child in turn. Have the child taste a salty item, a sour item, and a sweet item. After each taste, ask, "How does that taste?" The child should label the taste of all three food items correctly. If the child names the item instead of describing the taste, say "Yes, it's a _____ ; tell us how it tastes." Vary the order (sweet, sour, salty) and the items for each child.

Lesson 5—*(Introductory)* Touching

Objective—To identify an object as rough or smooth, using only the sense of touch

Materials—

Mirror and four other smooth objects
Piece of sandpaper and four other rough objects
Ball
Miniature animal
Ten objects with distinct shapes
Four rough objects
Four smooth objects
Blindfold

Procedure—

1. "Today we're going to talk about our sense of touch and some words we can use to tell how things feel."

2. Show the ball and the miniature animal. "Look at these two things. By using our eyes, we can tell that this one is a *(ball)* and that this one is an *(animal)*. But even if we couldn't see them, we probably could figure out what they were by touching them with our hands. I'm going to blindfold Tom, and we'll see if he can tell us which one is the ball just by feeling the objects." Blindfold the child. Hand the child the objects. Ask the child to hand you the ball.

3. Give each child a turn. Introduce two objects with distinct but different shapes, and have the child name the objects. Then blindfold the

child, hand the child the two objects, and call for one of the two.

4. "We know now that we can tell what things are by touching them. This time we'll play a game. I'll blindfold one of you and ask you to tell who someone is by touching that person. Look closely at all the people here." Give each child a turn to be blindfolded. Have the child stand. Have another child face the blindfolded child. Help the blindfolded child touch the other child's face, hair, and clothing in order to guess who the child is.

5. "There are lots of other things we can learn by touching and feeling. We can tell if things are hot or cold, dull or sharp, hard or soft, wet or dry, rough or smooth. Let's feel some of these things and decide if they are rough or smooth."

   a. Show the mirror. "What is this?" Give each child a chance to feel it. "Is it rough or smooth?" Show the sandpaper. "What is this?" Give each child a chance to feel it. "Is it rough or smooth?" Discuss these answers in greater detail if the children are unfamiliar with the words.

   b. "That time, we used our hands to feel the mirror and the sandpaper; but we could use any part of our bodies that has skin on it to feel if something is rough or smooth. We usually use our hands, but our skin can be used because our skin is a part of our sense of touch." Have the children rub the mirror and the sandpaper on their faces, arms, and legs, and state whether objects feel rough or smooth.

6. Provide the four rough and four smooth objects for the children to label as rough or smooth by feeling them with their hands and skin.

7. Blindfold each child in turn. Place two objects (one rough and one smooth) on the table. Help the child to grasp and feel the objects. "One of these is smooth, and one is rough. Hand me the rough one."

Lesson 6—*(Introductory)* Smelling

Objective—To identify three foods, using only the sense of smell

Materials—

Sliced onion	Fresh bread
Dill pickle	Banana partially peeled
Peanut butter	Perfume or scented soap
Small bottle filled with	Glue or paste
nontoxic household paint	

Procedure—

1. "Today we're not going to use our eyes" (point to eyes), "and we're not going to use our ears" (point to ears), "and we're not going to use our tongues" (point to tongue), "and we're not going to use our hands" (point to each hand). We're going to learn about our noses!" (point to nose)

2. "What can we learn by using our noses? Let's see. Everyone, close your eyes tight. I am going to hold something under your nose. Don't say anything; but if you know what is, raise your hand. Remember, keep your eyes closed, and don't say anything." Hold the onion under each child's nose. When all have had a turn to smell it, say "Don't open your eyes. Tell me what I held

under your nose." After the children have responded, tell them to open their eyes and see if their answers were correct. "How did you know it was an onion? Yes, you smelled it."

3. Using the same procedure with each item, have the children attempt to identify by smell.

4. "We know now that by using just our noses and smelling, we can tell what some things are. We can smell some things because they have an odor—a smell. Lots of times you can tell what's going on by using your nose to smell before you are able to use your eyes to see what's going on. For instance, when you go home and open the door, you might be able to *smell* that your mother is cooking supper before you walk into the kitchen and *see* that she is cooking." Have the children try to think of other instances in which they might know by smelling rather than seeing *(the grass being cut, the house being painted, mother using perfume for a party, . . .).*

5. If time permits, take the children on a walk around the school building or outside. Have them try to identify smells as they walk around *(food cooking in the kitchen or cafeteria, grass being cut, exhaust from a bus going by, odor from garbage cans, . . .).*

Lesson 7—*(Reinforcement)* Associating Body Parts with Senses

Objective—To identify body parts used for the senses

Materials—

The Senses Cards—one set for each child
(See preparation instructions below)

Tagboard
Glue
Scissors
Picture of a child
(See preparation instructions below)
Black crayons—one for each child

Preparing the materials —

1. Reproduce the Senses Cards (page 16). Make two copies for each child. Glue each copy onto tagboard. Cut apart into cards. Use one set as playing cards, and the other set as master cards. (Variation: The game can be made by using magazine pictures of eyes, ears, tongues, noses, and hands.)

2. Reproduce the picture of a child (page 15). Make a copy for each child in the group.

Procedure —

1. Give each child the picture of a child and a crayon.
   a. "Use your crayon and mark what we use to see."
   b. "Use your crayon and mark what we use to hear."
   c. "Use your crayon and mark what we use to smell."
   d. "Use your crayon and mark what we use to taste."
   e. "Use your crayon and mark what we use to feel."

2. Collect papers and crayons.

3. Give each child a master Senses card. Randomly spread the cards face up in the center of the table. "I am going to name one of the senses.

When you know what we use for that sense, find a picture in the middle of the table and cover that picture on your card."
   a. "Hearing is one of the senses. Find the picture that shows what we use to hear." Allow the children to locate and place the ear pictures on their master cards. Use the same procedure for the remaining cards.
   b. "Tasting is one of the senses. Find the picture that shows what we use to taste."
   c. "Seeing is one of the senses. Find the picture that shows what we use to see."
   d. "Feeling is one of the senses. Find the picture that shows what we use to feel."
   e. "Smelling is one of the senses. Find the picture that shows what we use to smell."
   f. "Find the missing picture for your card." Allow the children to locate and place the car pictures on their master cards. "What is it? Does it have anything to do with our senses? Is it a part of our bodies? Does it help us smell, feel, hear, see, or taste?"

4. "Let's name our senses once more. We have a sense of _____ , a sense of _____ , a sense of _____ , a sense of _____ , and a sense of _____ ." Help the children recall the five senses by providing clues if necessary.

Lesson 8—*(Reinforcement)*
Using the Senses

Objective —To point to the part of the body one uses to find out if something has an odor, how something tastes, what color it is, how it sounds, and how it feels

Materials —

Wooden block	Perfumed soap
Lemon slices	Red rubber ball
Record and	Cotton ball
record player	Dish of salt
Five sticker pictures	Paper
for each child	

Procedure —

1. "There are some words that we use when we talk about our senses. Today we'll use some of those words."

2. "Close your eyes. I'm holding a ball. Don't look! Is it red or green? Can you tell? Why not? Open your eyes. Is it red or green?" (If the children are not able to label colors, tell them the color of the ball.) "How do you know? Yes, we use our eyes to tell what color things are. If our eyes are closed, we can't see the colors. So *color* is a word we use when we talk about seeing with our eyes. Point to the part of your body you would use

to tell if something were yellow or brown." If necessary, explain again that without our eyes we can't see yellow and brown. "Yellow and brown are words we know about by using our eyes."

3. Place the wooden block and the cotton ball on the table. "Put your hands on your lap. Look at this block. Is it hard or soft? What would be the best way to find out? Yes, to touch it or feel it. Look at this cotton. Is it hard or soft? What would be the best way to find out?" Let the children handle the objects and conclude that the block is hard and the cotton is soft. "How do you know for sure that the block is hard? How do you know for sure that the cotton is soft? Yes, we used our hands to feel if they were hard or soft. So *hard* and *soft* are words we use when we talk about feeling with our hands. Point to the part of your body you use to tell if something is hard or soft." If necessary, again explain the association between feeling things that are hard and soft and our hands.

4. Continue this discussion, using the other materials.

   a. Place a lemon slice and the dish of salt on the table. "Look at this piece of lemon. Is it sour or salty? Look at this salt. Is it sour or salty? What would be the best way to find out?" After the children respond, have them taste the lemons and the salt. Conclude. "The lemon is sour; the salt is salty. We know because we tasted them with our tongues. *Sour* and *salty* are words we use when we talk about tasting with our tongues. Point to the part of your body you use to tell if something is sour or salty."

   b. Have the children hold their hands over their ears. Move your lips as if you were speaking normally, but whisper. "Hello, boys and girls." Direct the children to uncover their ears. "Did I speak loudly or quietly? Why couldn't you tell? That's right, you couldn't tell that I was whispering because your ears were covered."

   "Now I'll play a record. You tell me if the music is loud or quiet." Play the record so the music is barely audible. "Was it loud or quiet? How did you know?" Play the record again, turning the volume to loud. "Was the music loud or quiet that time? How did you know?" Conclude. "The music was loud one time and quiet one time. We know because we could hear it with our ears. *Loud* and *quiet* are words we use when we talk about listening with our ears. Point to the part of your body you use to tell if something is loud or quiet."

   c. Have the children pinch their noses closed with their fingers. Place the perfumed soap and the paper on the table. "Look at this soap. Does it have an odor or a smell? Look at this paper. Does it have an odor or a smell? What would be the best way to find out?" After the children respond, let them smell these items. Conclude. "The soap has an odor; the paper does not have an odor. We know because we smelled them with our noses. *Odor* is a word we use when we talk about smelling with our noses. Point to the part of your body you use to tell if something has an odor."

5. Review. Point to your nose. "We used our noses to find out if something had an <u>(odor)</u>." Point to your tongue. "We used our tongue to find out if something was <u>(sour)</u> or <u>(salty)</u>." Point to your hands. "We used our hands to find out if something was <u>(hard)</u> or <u>(soft)</u>." Point to your ears. "We used our ears to find out if something was <u>(loud)</u> or <u>(quiet)</u>." Point to your eyes. "We used our eyes to find out if something was <u>(red)</u> or <u>(green)</u>."

6. Give each child five sticker pictures.

   a. "Put a sticker on the part of your body you would use to find out if something were salty or sour."
   b. "Put a sticker on the part of your body you would use to find out if something were red or yellow."
   c. "Put a sticker on the part of your body you would use to find out if something were hard or soft."
   d. "Put a sticker on the part of your body you would use to find out if something were loud or quiet."
   e. "Put a sticker on the part of your body you would use to find out if something had an odor."

Lesson 9—*(Reinforcement)*
Identifying Objects with the Senses

Objective—To use the senses to identify objects

Materials—One of each for each child:

Marshmallows	Metal spoons
Orange slices	Blindfold
Raw carrot strips	

Procedure—

1. "It's easy for us to know what something is by looking at it with our eyes, isn't it? What are some of the other senses we could use to learn about things?" Use questions to help the children to recall the other four senses. "How do we know if something is hot or cold? How do we know if something has an odor?"

2. "Now we'll play a game called Fun with All Our Senses. Do you think we can use more than one of our senses at the same time? Can we *see* and *hear* at the same time? Yes. Can we *feel* and *taste* at the same time? Yes. Can we *feel* and *see* and *hear* and *taste* and *smell* all at the same time? Yes! Most of the time we use all the senses we can, to find out about things."

3. Blindfold the children. "When I blindfold your eyes, what sense am I covering up? If I give you something, will you be able to see what it is? What other senses could you use to find out what it is?" As the game proceeds and the children make guesses, do not tell them if they are correct or incorrect. Just remind them they will use *all* their senses to decide what the object is.

   a. Place a marshmallow in each child's hand. "I'm handing you something. Use just your sense of touch—feel it and see if you can tell what it is. How does it feel? What do you think it is?"

   b. "Now use your sense of hearing—use your ears. Does the thing I gave you make any sounds? What do you think it is?"

   c. "Now use your sense of smell—use your nose. Does the thing I gave you have an odor? What do you think it is?"

   d. "Now, because what I gave you can be eaten, use your sense of taste—your tongue. Take just one bite. How does it taste? What do you think it is?"

   e. "Now take off the blindfold and use your sense of sight—use your eyes to see if you were right. What is it?"

   f. Review. "We used many of our senses to learn that was a marshmallow.
   Could you *feel* it was a marshmallow?
   Could you *hear* it was a marshmallow?
   Could you *smell* it was a marshmallow?
   Could you *taste* it was a marshmallow?
   Could you *see* it was a marshmallow?"

4. Follow the same procedure with the other materials. In turn, blindfold each child, and hand the child an item to be identified. Have the child feel and guess, hear and guess, smell and guess, and taste and guess. (Although the children cannot "eat" the spoon, they can "taste" it by placing it in their mouths.) Have each child look and check the correctness of the guesses. Review as in #3f, above.

Lesson 10—*(Extension)*
Combining Senses

Objective—To tell what information can be obtained about the object using two different senses

Materials—Box containing:

Gumdrop	Block	Pretzel
Slice of onion	Bell	Orange
Small red rubber ball		

Procedure—

1. "We've talked about all our senses now. We've used our eyes to (see), we've used our ears to (hear), we've used our hands to (feel), we've used our tongues to (taste), and we've used our noses to (smell)."

2. "Usually we use some or all of our senses together. By using all our senses, we can learn more about things." Show the rubber ball. "I can

use my senses to learn about this ball, for instance. I can *see* that it's round and that it's red. When I bounce it, I can *hear* it bounce. If I touch it, I can *feel* its shape; I can squeeze it, too. The only sense I don't use is my sense of taste, because the ball isn't food."

3. "Today, we'll go on a walk to see what we can learn by using our senses." Take the children for a walk inside or outside the building. "When you hear something, or smell something, or feel something, or see something, let us know. We'll stop and talk about which of your senses you are using." As the children make observations ("I hear a car; I see a tree"), discuss each in terms of the senses used to make the observation.

   a. Restate the child's remark. "Joe says he *sees* a tree. He is using his eyes. Can you all see the tree with your eyes?"

   b. "Can we *hear* the tree with our ears?" If it's windy, the children may be able to hear the wind in the tree.

   c. "Can we *feel* the tree?" Have the children feel the bark of the tree. If the branches are low enough, the children can touch the leaves or needles and branches.

   d. "Can we *taste* the tree?"

   e. "Can we *smell* the tree?" In the spring the tree might have blossoms or a "green" smell. Evergreen needles are fragrant.

   f. Conclude. "Joe knew that was a tree because he saw it with his eyes. But we learned more about the tree by using our ears to listen to the sound it made, our hands to feel it, and our noses to smell it."

After each child has made at least one observation, return to the classroom.

4. Show the children the box containing the materials listed above. "I'm going to tell you something about an object in this box. Then I want you to tell me two senses I could have used to know what I told you." Show the rubber ball. "This ball is round. How do I know that it is round? Yes, I can see that it is round, but I can also feel that the ball is round." If the children seem confused, give a second example using the pretzel. Take the pretzel out of the box and take a bite. "This is a pretzel. How do I know this is a pretzel? What two senses could I use? Yes, I can *see* that it's a pretzel and I can *taste* that it's a pretzel."

   a. Ring the bell. "This is a bell. How do I know this is a bell? What two senses could I use?" *(see, hear)*

   b. Show the slice of onion. "This is an onion. How do I know this is an onion? What senses could I use?" *(see, taste, smell)*

   c. Show the block. "This is a block. How do I know this is a block? What two senses could I use?" *(see, feel)*

   d. Show the gumdrop. "This is a gumdrop. How do I know this is a gumdrop? What two senses could I use?" *(see, taste)*

   e. Show the orange. "This is an orange. How do I know this is an orange? What senses could I use?" *(see, feel, smell, taste)*.

Lesson 11—*(Extension)* Listening

Objective—To follow directions and respond according to directions

Materials—

Tape recorder
Sound tape (See preparation instructions below)
Dish containing pretzel sticks broken in half
Napkins—one for each child

Preparing the tape—Prepare the tape before the lesson.

1. Assign a number to each child in the group. When the sequence outlined below is recorded, each child's name will be heard twice on the tape.

2. Record a variety of music (marches, songs, lullabies) and imitate animal sounds ("oink-oink"

and "meow"). Include a five-second interval between each designated sound. Make the sound tape three to five minutes long.

3. Record the material in the following sequence: Name of child 1, name of child 3, music, animal sound, name of child 5, music, name of child 1, music, animal sound, animal sound, name of child 2, music, music, animal sound, name of child 3, name of child 4, animal sound, music, name of child 2, music, animal sound, name of child 5, name of child 4.

Procedure—

1. "We're going to play a game where we'll listen for special sounds. What part of our bodies will we use to listen? We'll listen for our names sometimes, for music sometimes, and for animal sounds sometimes. When you hear what you are supposed to be listening for, you may take a pretzel and put it on your napkin. Don't eat the pretzel! We'll all eat them later."

2. "Before we start, let's practice. I'll say some things. If you hear your name, you may take a pretzel."

   a. Say one child's name. If necessary, remind the child to take a pretzel.

   b. "This time if you hear music, you may take a pretzel." Hum a tune and then ask, "Is that music? Should you take a pretzel? Why? Right! That time you may take a pretzel if you hear music."

   c. "If you hear an animal sound, take a pretzel. Oink-oink. You all took a pretzel because you heard an animal sound. Very good!"

   d. Continue practicing until the children are able to follow these directions easily.

3. "Now we'll listen to lots of sounds. There will be one sound after another. This time, whenever you hear *your* name, you may take a pretzel. Listen carefully." Play the tape and help the children as needed. At the end of the tape, each child should have two pretzels.

4. Rewind the tape. Instruct the children to take a pretzel whenever they hear music. Play the tape again. Give help as needed.

5. Rewind the tape. Instruct the children to take a pretzel whenever they hear an animal sound. Play the tape again. Give help as needed.

The Senses

The Senses Cards

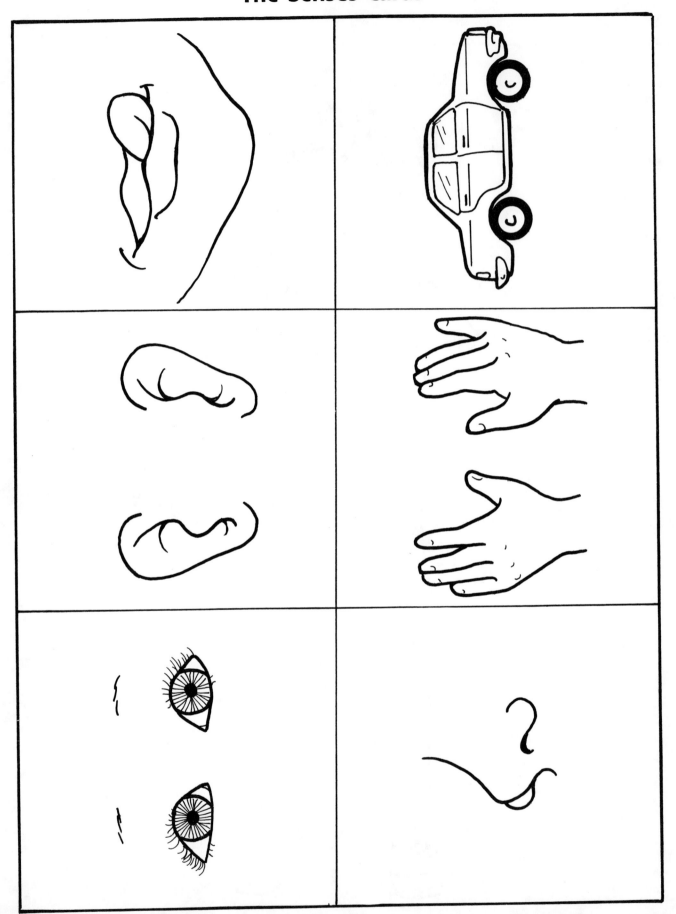

Unit II
Air

Language Development—
Goals, Objectives, and Vocabulary

Goals

To develop an understanding of the relationships among air, our senses, and the surrounding environment

To review the senses and their relationship to air

Objectives

Receptive

The student will:

1. Identify body parts with appropriate sense

2. Comprehend the difference between *inhale* and *exhale*

3. Associate the movements of objects with the wind

4. Follow given directions and successfully construct two items (a fan and a pinwheel)

Expressive

The student will:

1. Label body parts with appropriate sense

2. Respond to yes/no questions related to the senses and the perception of air

3. Identify characteristics of air as they relate to the senses (feel it, see it, hear it, . . .)

4. Combine information and express a solution to a given problem related to the senses and air

5. Describe the movements caused by wind as observed (bending tree branches, blowing paper, floating, . . .)

Vocabulary

air	alive	whole
breathe	dead	through
fear	pull	pinwheel
feel	push	wind
breathing	filled	fluttering
inhale	empty	bending
exhale	all	blowing

Lesson 1—*(Introductory)*
Air All Around Us

Objective—To demonstrate an understanding that air is all around us

Materials—

Empty plastic liquid soap bottle with removable lid and spout

Paper fan pattern (See preparation instructions below)

Construction paper

Paper clips—one for each child

Preparing the materials—Reproduce the paper fan pattern (page 26) on construction paper. Make a copy for each child. Trim the patterns. The children will fold the paper along the dotted lines and place the paper clip at the lower end to keep the fan from unfolding.

Procedure—

1. Review the senses. "We've learned lots of things about our senses. We've used our eyes to see, our ears to hear, and our skin and hands to feel. We've used our noses to smell and our tongues to taste. Today, and every day from now on, we'll use our senses to learn about all kinds of things. As we work, think about the senses you are using to learn what you're learning."

2. Show the empty plastic bottle. "This is a soap bottle, but I've taken out all the soap." Remove the top of the bottle and give each child a chance to inspect the inside. "Use your sense of sight and look inside the bottle. Do you *see* anything inside?" Conclude. "No, our eyes can't see anything inside the bottle." Turn the bottle upside down. "When we turn the bottle upside down, we can't *see* anything come out, can we?"

3. "But there *is* something in the bottle. It is something we can't see. What's in the bottle doesn't have an odor, so we can't smell it. It's not something we eat, so we can't taste it. But get your

sense of touch ready, because we can *feel* what's in the bottle! And if we are very quiet we might be able to *hear* what's in the bottle."

4. Put the lid back on the bottle and open the spout. Hold the spout near each child's face and squeeze the bottle so the children can feel the air and hear it come out. "Can you feel something? Can you hear it? What is in the bottle, that comes out when I squeeze it? Yes, there is air in the bottle. How do we know? Could we see it? Could we taste it? Could we smell it? Could we hear it? Could we feel it?"

5. "We know air is in the bottle. Let's see if we can discover where else there is air." Instruct the children to fan their hands in front of their faces. "Can you feel anything? Do you suppose there's air in front of your face? Can you see it? Can you hear it? Can you feel it?"

6. Give each child a paper fan pattern and a paper clip. "So far, we know air was in the bottle and air was in front of our faces. Now we'll make fans. With our fans, we'll be able to feel where there is air in the room." Help each child to fold the paper and place a paper clip at the lower end to keep the fan from unfolding.

7. "Let's see if there is still air in front of our faces. Everyone, move your fan in front of your face. Is there still air there? How do you know?" Have the children fan their legs, arms, chests, feet. Conclude. "Air is all around our bodies."

8. "Let's look around the room and find out where else there is air." Have the children take turns going to various places in the room and fanning to see if there is air in that part of the room. Give each child specific directions. "Sarah, go over to the bookshelf and fan yourself." Ask, "Is there air over there? How do you know? Can you see it?" Give each child at least one turn. Conclude. "There was air in the bottle, air in front of our faces, air over by the bookshelves, (and so on). Air is everywhere, isn't it? It's all around us."

Lesson 2—*(Introductory)* Air in Our Bodies

Objective—To demonstrate an understanding that all people have air in their bodies

Materials—

Balloons—one for each child and one for the teacher

Hand mirrors—one for each child

Procedure—

1. "Yesterday we learned there is air all around our bodies and all around the room. There's another place where there is air, and I'll bet you'll be surprised to learn about it! Watch." Take out a balloon and blow it up. Squeeze the end shut. "What did I put in the balloon to make it get bigger?" Hold the balloon next to a child's hand and release the end so some air will escape against the child's hand. "What is coming out of the balloon? Can you see it? Can you hear it? Can you feel it?" Give each child a turn to feel the air escaping from the balloon.

2. "We decided that the balloon got bigger because I put air in it. We could feel and hear the air coming out of the balloon. Now watch carefully, and tell me where I get the air that I put in the balloon." Blow up the balloon again. "Where did I get the air that I put in the balloon? Yes, the air was in my body and I blew it into the balloon. Do you suppose you have air in your body? I'll give each of you a balloon." Help each child to blow up a balloon and then to release the end and feel the air come out. "Do you all have air in your bodies?"

3. "There are other ways we can know that we have air in our bodies."

   a. "If we blow on our hands" (demonstrate), "we can feel the air." Have the children blow on their hands. "Can you see the air coming from your body? Can you hear the air coming from your body? Can you feel the air coming from your body? Do you all have air in your bodies?"

   b. "We can close our mouths and put air in them like this." Close your mouth and puff up your cheeks by filling them with air. Have the children do the same. "We can't see the air, but we know it's there because we can see our cheeks getting bigger just like the balloon did." Give each child a hand mirror. Have the children look at their cheeks as they fill them with air. Have them look at other children's cheeks also. "Do you all have air in your bodies?"

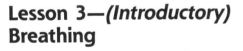

Lesson 3—*(Introductory)* Breathing

Objective—To interpret inhaling and exhaling as breathing

Procedure—

1. "We've learned that there is air all around our bodies and air inside our bodies. Today we'll talk about how we breathe by using the air outside our bodies and the air inside our bodies."

2. "Everyone, take a deep breath and bring lots of air into your body." Demonstrate and have the children imitate. "Now let all the air out." Demonstrate and have the children imitate. Repeat at least three times.

3. Review. "What did we just do? Yes, we took air into our bodies and we let air out of our bodies. When we take air in, let air out, take air in, let air out, take air in—we call that *breathing*. Let's all say that word together—*breathing*. We breathe all the time, even though we aren't thinking about it. If we stopped breathing, we'd die. In order to be alive and to move and to talk and to walk and to play, we have to breathe. What is it that we breathe? Yes, air. If we didn't have air to breathe, we wouldn't be able to stay alive."

4. "Breathing is very important, so we'll spend some time today learning about breathing. First, there are some words you should know. When we take air in, we *inhale*. Let's all say that—*inhale*. When we let air out, we *exhale*. Let's all say that—*exhale*.

Now let's practice inhaling and exhaling. Take air in—inhale, let air out—exhale, take air in—inhale, let air out—exhale." Pause for a moment, since breathing deeply for an extended period may cause dizziness. "Inhale, exhale, inhale, exhale, inhale, exhale." Pause again. Continue having the children practice until they are able to follow the directions.

5. Ask each child, "What do we do when we breathe?" or "How do we breathe?" If necessary, remind the child that we inhale (take air in) and exhale (let air out).

6. Ask the group, "*What* do we breathe?" *(air)* If the children cannot answer, ask, "Do we breathe water? Do we breathe milk? Do we breathe air?"

7. "If we put our hands on our chests, we can feel the air going in and out of our bodies." Help the children place their hands appropriately. "Everyone, inhale. What happens when we inhale? Yes, our chests get larger as the air goes in." Have the children feel this effect several times. "Everyone, inhale. Your chest is bigger, isn't it? Now exhale. What happens when we exhale? Right, your chest gets smaller as the air goes out." Have the children feel this effect several times.

Lesson 4—*(Reinforcement)* Moving Things with Air

Objective—To apply the principle of air movement to solve a problem which involves moving an object without touching it

Materials—
Newspaper, torn into 1" squares
Plastic bottle (from Lesson 1)
Paper fans (from Lesson 1)—one for each child
Small paper cup
Cardboard, 8½" x 11"
Shoebox

Procedure—

1. Show the bottle. "Remember when we talked about this bottle? We said there was something in the bottle that we couldn't see, but we could feel it if we squeezed the bottle. What's inside the bottle? Yes, air. Now I'm going to open my mouth and I want you to look inside. What do you see in there? Yes, my tongue and my teeth and the inside of my cheeks. But there's something in there that we can't see. If I blow on my hand" (demonstrate), "I can feel it. What is in my mouth that you can't see?" *(air)*

2. "We already know several things about air. For instance, we know we breathe air. What else do we know about air?" Give the children time to recall other information. *(Air is all around us, air is in our bodies, we can't see air but we can feel air.)*

Supply any information the children fail to mention. "Today we'll learn something new about air. We'll learn that air can move things."

3. Put some of the newspaper scraps on the table. Hold up the plastic bottle. "Suppose I wanted to move these paper scraps without touching them with my hands. What is in this bottle that could move the paper scraps?" Aim the bottle at the paper scraps, squeeze the bottle, and let the stream of air move the paper. Give each child a turn to move the paper with the airstream from the bottle. Review. "How did we move the paper pieces?" Conclude. "Air can move and push things." Remove the bottle.

4. Give each child a paper fan. Place a small pile of paper scraps in front of each child. "Don't touch the paper. Use your fan and move the paper pieces. What moved the paper? Yes, your fan made the air move, and the air moved the paper." Have each child fan paper scraps into the empty shoebox. Remove the scraps and collect the fans.

5. Give each child another pile of paper scraps. "Don't touch the paper. Think very hard about how you could move the paper without touching it with any part of your body. When you think you know how you could do it, raise your hand." Two possibilities should be suggested by the children: you can use air from your body and blow on the paper pieces; you can fan your hand back and forth above the paper pieces. If no

child can think of a way to solve the problem, offer clues but do not tell the solution. Remind them, "We've been using air to move the paper. Where can we find some air? If we make the air move, then the paper will move because the air will push it. How can we make the air move?" Continue to assist the children until both possibilities have been discovered. Let each child practice moving the paper by each method. Review. "How did we move the paper?" *(By making air move which pushed the paper; by using air.)*

Lesson 5—(Reinforcement) Air Takes Up Space

Objective—To demonstrate an understanding that air must be removed before an object can be filled with water

Materials—

Small transparent paper or plastic cup (See preparation instructions below)

Transparent bowl (See preparation instructions below)

Preparing the materials—

1. Punch a ¼″ hole in the bottom of the cup.

2. Fill the bowl with enough water to cover the cup when it is submerged.

Procedure—

1. Have the children stand up, put their hands on their chests, and feel their chests get larger as they inhale and smaller as they exhale. "Our chests get larger when we inhale because we take air in. When we exhale and let the air out again, our chests get smaller. That's because air takes up space even though we can't see it. Today we'll do some experiments to show that air takes up space."

2. Show the children the cup with the hole in the bottom. "What is this? Yes, it's a cup, and it has a hole in the bottom. What is in the cup?" *(air)* Show the bowl containing water. "What is this? What's in the bowl?" *(water)*

6. Work individually with each child at a distance from the group. Place the paper cup on its side on a level table. Place the cardboard on the table. "I have a problem for you. I want you to move this paper cup without touching it with any part of your body. You may use this piece of cardboard if you want to, but don't touch the cup with the cardboard. Think about what we've learned today. Now, move the cup but don't touch it!" The child may move the cup by fanning it with the hands, by fanning it with the cardboard, or by blowing at the cup.

3. "We said this cup has air in it, and we said air takes up space. Let's see what happens if I put this cup of air into the water." Invert the cup, holding it straight up and down so that the rim of the cup will enter the water first. Place your thumb tightly over the hole to prevent any air from escaping from the cup. Slowly submerge the cup into the water. "Look carefully. Did the water go into the cup? No, the water could not go into the cup because there already is something in the cup. What is in the cup? Yes, air. That air is taking up space in the cup and there isn't any room for water to get in. We must let the air out of the cup to make room for the water. Now watch. I'll take my finger off the hole in the cup so the air can come out." Remove your finger. The air will escape from the cup and cause bubbles in the water. At the same time, the children will be able to see the water rising in the cup. "Do you see the air coming out of the cup? See the bubbles? Those are bubbles of air. As the air comes out of the hole in the cup, what goes into the cup? Yes, water. We let the air out and now there is room for the water." Repeat this experiment several times so the children can see the water replacing the air. Discuss as you repeat the experiment. "Air takes up space. As long as there is air in the cup, there is no room for water. When the air is let out of the cup, there is room for water, and water fills the cup. You can see the air leaving the cup in bubbles as the water goes in."

4. Let the children take turns performing variations on this experiment. In each case, discuss why water did or did not go into the cup.

    a. "Put the cup in the water, but don't let any water go into the cup." The child must cover the hole in the cup with one thumb.

    b. "Put the cup in the water slowly so we can see the water going into the cup." The child submerges the cup without covering the hole.

    c. "Put the cup in the water, but don't let any water go into the cup. Now, let the water in." The child holds a thumb over the hole until the cup is submerged, then removes the thumb.

Lesson 6—(Reinforcement) Exchanging Air for a Liquid

Objective—To remove air from a straw and replace it with juice, and to remove juice from a straw and replace it with air

Materials—

Transparent cups—two for each child and one for the teacher

Transparent plastic straws—two for each child and one for the teacher

Pitcher of juice

Procedure—

1. "Yesterday we talked about air and learned that air takes up space. Now, that's very difficult to remember. We can't see air, so we have a hard time remembering that it takes up space. Today we'll do some more experiments with air to help us remember."

2. Show a drinking straw. "What is this? What is inside the straw?" *(air)* Fill a cup with juice. "What is this? What is inside the cup?" *(juice)*

3. "Watch what happens when I put the straw in the juice." Slowly lower the straw into the juice. Have the children observe that as the straw goes into the juice, it begins to fill with juice. "We said there was air in the straw. We know air takes up space. If there is already air in the straw, how is it the juice can get in?" *(The air is leaving the straw through the open end.)* "Watch what happens if I hold the end of the straw closed so the air can't get out. Do you think there will be any room for the juice?" Put your thumb over the end of the straw, and lower it into the juice. No

juice enters the straw. "Why didn't the juice go into the straw? Right, there wasn't room. The straw had air in it, and the air couldn't get out because my thumb was over the end of the straw."

4. Give each child a cup of juice and a straw. Have the children perform the following experiments.

    a. "Put your straw in the juice. What happened? Why?"

    b. "Hold your finger over the end of the straw. Put your straw in the juice. What happened? Why?"

5. "Now put your straw in the juice again. What is in your straw now? Yes, some juice and some air. Suppose we want to fill the *whole* straw with juice. What will we have to do? Yes, we'll have to take out *all* the air so there will be room for the juice. How can we do that? We can suck the air out." Have the children watch each other take sips of juice and observe the air going out as the juice comes into the straw. "Everyone, stop sucking the air out of the straw. Everyone, stop drinking juice. What happens when we stop? Right, air goes into the straw again."

6. "This time, let's fill the whole straw with air. How could we do that? We could blow the juice out of the straw by blowing air into the straw." Have the children take turns watching each other blow gently through the straw and observing the juice leaving the straw as the air fills the straw. "Why does the juice go out of our straws when we blow air into them? Yes, there isn't room for juice *and* air because both take up space." Discuss the bubbles. "As you blow more and more air into the straw, where does the air go? It goes into the juice. How do you know the air is going into

the juice? Right, because you can see bubbles of air in the juice."

Lesson 7—*(Extension)* Wind

This lesson must be done on a breezy or windy day.

Objective—To identify evidences of wind

Materials—

Cardboard, 8½″ x 11″
Electric fan
Wind and No Wind Pictures
(See preparation instructions below)

Preparing the materials—

Reproduce the Wind and No Wind Pictures (pages 27-29). Color the pictures and mount them on construction paper.

Procedure—

1. "We already know that air can move things." Review how air moved paper scraps in various ways (fanning with your hand, fanning with a fan, blowing). Explain that when air moves, we call it *wind*.

2. Ask the children to blow on their hands. "Can you feel the wind? Can you feel the air moving?"

3. "Usually there is no wind inside buildings or rooms, unless we make a wind. We can blow air and make a wind, like we just did. We can make a wind by fanning a piece of paper or cardboard." Demonstrate, letting each child feel the wind. "We can use an electric fan to make a wind." Demonstrate. "There are lots of ways to make wind. All we have to do is move the air."

4. "Outside, the air moves all around. Let's go outside and see if there is any wind today. Pretend

7. Give the children time to experiment independently. Visit with each child to discuss what is happening.

you are photographers taking pictures of the wind." Take the children outside. "Is there any wind today? Is the air moving? How do you know? Yes, you can see the air is moving things. What are some of the things the air is moving?" Help the children to notice the movement of leaves on trees or pieces of paper, to feel the wind on their faces, to notice how it blows their hair or the smoke from a chimney. Tell the children, "Pretend you are photographing the objects that are being moved by the air."

5. Bring the children back into the classroom. "Look out the window. Can you tell if there's wind outside just by *looking*? Yes, because you can see things the wind is moving. When we were outside, we could feel the wind and see the things it moved. Inside, we can only see the things it moves." Let the children pretend to photograph things moved by the air.

6. Present the Wind and No Wind pictures. "We can tell when we look at pictures if there is wind in the picture. Even though we can't *feel* the wind in a picture, there are things in the picture that give us clues and tell us it is windy. Let's look at these pictures and decide if it is windy or not." Discuss the visual clues on each of the pictures. *(Leaves blowing off a tree, people's clothing or hair blowing in one direction, a flag fluttering, smoke floating off in one direction.)* Show each child a picture showing evidence of wind and one showing no evidence of wind. Ask the child to point to the windy picture.

Lesson 8—(Extension)
Observing Wind

Objective—To use several methods to make a pinwheel turn

Materials—

Pinwheel pattern
  (See preparation instructions below)
Construction paper
Scissors
Unsharpened pencil with eraser for each child
Straight pin for each child
Tape
Electric fan

Preparing the materials—

Photocopy the pinwheel pattern (page 30) on construction paper. Cut along the dotted lines. Make one for each child.

Procedure—

1. Help each child construct a pinwheel.
   a. Tape the tip of each corner marked "x", one at a time, on the "x" in the center circle.
   b. Place the straight pin through the center of the paper pinwheel and then through the eraser on the pencil. The pencil serves as a handle for the pinwheel.

2. "Now everyone has a pinwheel. Push your pinwheel with your hand. You can move it." Demonstrate this movement.

3. "We know there is something all around us that we can use to move things. What is it? Yes, air can move things. Do you suppose we could move our pinwheels by making the air move? Let's see. Will the pinwheels move if we blow on them? Try it. Why did they move? We made the air move—we made a wind which caused our pinwheels to move."

4. Have the children try to move their pinwheels in other situations.
   a. In front of a fan which is turned off. "Why didn't the pinwheel move?"
   b. In front of a fan which is turned on. "Why did the pinwheel move?"
   c. Outside (if the weather is appropriate). "Why did (or didn't) the pinwheel move?"

Lesson 9—(Extension)
Musical Containers

This lesson deals with the concept of long and short columns of air. As the length of the columns of air in a glass is changed, different musical notes will be produced when the glass is struck.

This lesson may be used in conjunction with Unit IV, "Sound," rather than here. Some teachers may wish to use this lesson in both places with variations.

Objective—To predict whether two glasses containing unequal amounts of air will make the same sound when struck

Materials—

Five identical water glasses
Pitcher of water colored with food coloring
Five large nails
Measuring cup

Procedure—

1. Ask one child to stand in the farthest corner of the room and shout, "Hello, everybody!" Have the child return to the group. Discuss what happened. "When Joe was standing over there, he shouted 'Hello, everybody.' Could we hear him? Yes. But there was something between Joe and us—something we can't see. What was it? *(air)* Did the air stop the sound of his voice? No, the sound of his voice went through the air, from way over there to here, and we could hear his voice. That's because sounds can go through air. Air carries sounds."

2. "We're going to do an experiment today with sounds and air, and we'll discover that we can change a sound depending on how much air we use."

3. Show the children an empty glass. "What is in this glass?" *(air)* Have one child gently tap the

side of the glass with a nail. "What happened? Yes, it made a sound."

4. Place a second glass on the table and fill it with ½ cup of water. "What is in this glass?" *(some air, some water)* Have one child gently tap the side of the glass with a nail. "What happened? Right, again it made a sound."

5. Compare the sounds made by striking the two glasses. "We know this glass has air in it, and this glass has air and water in it. Which glass has the *most* air? We also know they both make a sound when we hit the glass. Let's listen again and see if the sounds are exactly the same." Have the children strike the glasses again and conclude that the sounds are not the same.

6. Show the third glass. "Let's see what sound we will get if we put even less air in this glass. If we want less air, we have to put in more *(water)*. We know that if we put water in the glass, some of the air will have to come out to make room for the water." Place the third glass next to the second and add one cup of water. "Which glass has the most air? Which glass has the least air? If we hit this glass," (the third glass) "do you think we'll hear a sound?" Have a child strike the third glass. Beginning with the first glass, compare the sounds made by striking each glass in turn. Help the children conclude that the sounds differ according to the amount of air in the glass.

7. Follow the same procedure until all five glasses are in a row on the table.
   a. Show the glass.
   b. "Let's have even less air in this glass. If we want less air, we have to put in more *(water)*."

c. Place the glass in line. Add one-half cup more water than was in the previous glass.
   d. "Which glass has the most air? Which glass has the least air?"
   e. "If we hit this glass, do you think we'll hear a sound?"
   f. Have a child strike the glass just added to the line.
   g. Beginning with the first glass, compare the sounds made by striking each glass in turn. Conclude. Sounds differ according to the amount of air in the glass.

8. Have five children sit in a row on one side of the table. Taking the glasses in order, place one glass in front of each child. Give each child a nail. Beginning with the child who has the glass that contains only air, have each child strike a glass in turn. Reverse the procedure, beginning with the child who has the glass that contains the least air. Repeat several times, and discuss how the sounds change. "When we start with the glass that has the most air and go to the glass with the least air, each sound gets *(higher)*. When we start with the glass that has the least air and go to the glass with the most air, each sound gets *(lower)*." Modulate your voice as you talk to indicate *higher* and *lower*. Although the children are not expected to remember this association, it should be explained to them. If they show interest in the lesson, a follow-up lesson can be done in which this association is stressed.

9. Review. Have the children strike the glasses in order at least three more times. Stress the idea that each sound is different because the amount of air in each glass is different.

Paper Fan Pattern

Wind and No Wind Pictures

27

Wind and No Wind Pictures

Wind and No Wind Pictures

Pinwheel Pattern

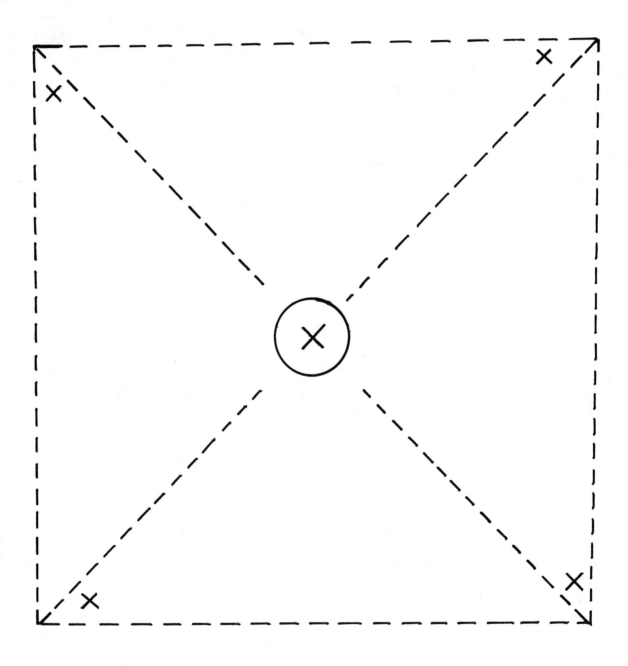

Unit III

Water

Language Development— Goals, Objectives, and Vocabulary

Goals

To develop an understanding of the concept of water and its functions

To associate water with its attributes and relationship to the environment

Objectives

Receptive

The student will:

1. Associate changes in color and taste with the addition of ingredients

2. Comprehend the concepts *same* and *different* and classify liquids as same and different according to color and taste

3. Recognize various forms of water (lake, faucet, ice, ...) and important uses of water (washing, drinking, fire fighting, ...)

4. Compare similarities and differences of three water forms (frozen, boiling, melting)

5. Identify melting, frozen, boiling water in a field of three

6. Comprehend meaning of *evaporation* in a given situation

7. Categorize items as *sinkers* or *floaters*

8. Comprehend and differentiate the meaning of *solid, liquid, gas*

9. Select a named form (*solid, liquid, gas*) from a vision field of three

Expressive

The student will:

1. Explain the meaning of *evaporation*

2. Comprehend the meaning of *sink* and *float* by stating whether objects sank or floated

3. Define the meaning of *sink* and *float* when identifying an object as a "sinker" or "floater"

Vocabulary

same	evaporate	gas
different	evaporation	ocean
small	sink	lake
smaller	float	underwater
melt	bottom	whale
freeze	top	octopus
steam	solid	starfish
boiling	liquid	

Lesson 1—*(Introductory)*
Using Water

Objective—To state one use for water

Materials—

Can of frozen lemonade

Paper cups—three for each child

Three pitchers (See preparation instructions below)

Envelope of soup broth mix

Preparing the materials—Fill one pitcher with enough cold water for each child to have a taste. Fill the second pitcher with the amount of cold water needed to make lemonade. Fill the third pitcher with the amount of very warm water needed to mix a package of soup broth.

Procedure—

1. Pour a cup of water for each child. "What is that? When you look at it with your eyes, what do you think it is? Now use another one of your senses. Taste it and see if you were right. What is it? Yes, it is water."

2. "We drink water often, don't we? Did you know that if we didn't have water to drink, we wouldn't be able to stay alive? Remember when we talked about air? Do we need air to stay alive? Yes, we have to have air to breathe and water to drink in order to stay alive."

3. "We can drink plain water just as we did a minute ago. But sometimes we use water to make different things to eat or drink. Did you ever see someone use water to make something to drink?" Discuss the children's suggestions.

4. Show the can of lemonade. "Here is something we can make with water. It's lemonade. Watch what happens when I put the lemonade in the water." Open the package and pour the lemonade into the pitcher of cold water. "What happened? Yes, we can see that the water is a different color now. Do you suppose the water will taste the same?" Pour a glass of lemonade for each child. "Does it taste the same? No, it tastes different because we added the lemonade to the water. The lemonade had a flavoring that made the water taste fruity, sugar that made the water taste sweet, and coloring that made the water change color."

5. Show the package of soup mix. "Here is something else we can add to water. Does anyone know what this is?" Open the envelope. "Watch what happens when I put the soup mix in the water." Pour in the soup mix. "What happened?" Discuss. "Do you suppose the water will taste different?" Give each child a sample. "Does it taste different? Why?"

6. "There are lots and lots of things we add water to in order to make food to eat. We use water to make cakes. We use water to make soup." Elicit suggestions from the group.

Lesson 2—*(Introductory)*
Water Pictures

Objective—To find pictures depicting uses for water

Materials—

Scissors for each child

Magazines

Cardboard or posterboard 36″ square

Paste

Preparing the materials—Before the lesson, collect magazines that contain water-related pictures— glasses of water, lakes, swimming pools, firemen fighting fires, clothes or dishes being washed, ice cubes, ice skating, and so on. Have two magazines available for each child and one for the teacher.

Procedure—

1. "Yesterday we talked about one way we use water. Who remembers what that was? *(eating, drinking)* What are some other ways we use water?" Discuss the children's ideas. If they offer none, suggest routines at bedtime (brushing teeth, bathing) and mealtime (washing dishes).

2. "There are lots of ways we use water. We are going to look in these magazines for pictures about water. We'll cut them out and paste them

on this big piece of cardboard. Let's look hard and see how many different water pictures we can find."

3. Page through a magazine while the children watch. When you find a water-related picture, say, "Here is a picture we can use for our chart. What are these people using water to do?" After you have cut two or three pictures, paste them on the chart.

Lesson 3—*(Introductory)*
Forms of Water

Objective—To distinguish among three forms of water—frozen, boiling, melting

Materials—

Dish of ice cubes
Refrigerator or freezer
Paper cups—one for each child
Pitcher of water
Marking pen
Hot plate or stove
Pan containing about one cup of water
Metal cup

Procedure—

1. "We've talked about ways in which we use water. Today we'll talk about the different forms water can have and how we can change its form."

2. Present an ice cube in a dish. "What is this? Yes, it's an ice cube. Does anyone know how we make ice cubes?" Accept the children's suggestions. Summarize. "If we take some water and put it in the freezer, it will get very, very cold. After awhile it will get hard like this ice cube. It will *freeze*. I'll give each of you a paper cup, and I'll write your name on it. Now we'll pour some water into the cups. We'll put them in the freezer, and we'll check later (or tomorrow) to see what's happened."

   Have the children check later to see the ice that forms. Conclude. "One thing we can do to water is *freeze* it. How do we freeze water? What happens when we freeze it?"

4. "Now I'll give each of you a magazine. When you find a picture having to do with water, cut it out and paste it on the chart." Discuss the pictures as the children discover them. Let the children work independently, but assist any child who has difficulty.

3. Return to the ice cube in the dish. "Oh, look what's happening to our ice cube!" Have the children discuss what is happening. *(The cube is getting smaller; the ice is turning into water.)* "When frozen water (ice) turns back into water, we say it *melts*. Can you say that word? The ice cube is melting because it is warm in the room. An ice cube cannot stay frozen unless it's kept in the freezer where it's very, very cold. When we take it out of the freezer, it begins to melt." Give each child a chip of ice. "Put the ice in your mouth. Don't swallow it; just put it on your tongue. What is happening? Yes, it's melting. Why is it melting?"

4. Turn on the hot plate. "This is a hot plate. I have turned it on, and it will get very hot." Have the children hold their hands over the burner to feel the heat, but caution them not to touch the burner.

   "Watch what happens when I put a pan of water on the hot plate. The pan and the water will get hot from the burner, so don't put your hand in the water or touch the pan. Just watch." Point out when bubbles begin to form and steam begins to escape. "When water gets very, very hot, it turns into steam. This" (point to steam) "is called *steam*." Have the children repeat the word. "When water is very hot like this and is turning to steam, we say it is *boiling*." Have the children repeat the word. "How can we make water boil?"

5. Review.

   a. Take two or three fresh ice cubes from the freezer. "What is this? How did I make the ice? Did I boil it, freeze it, or melt it?"

b. Place the ice cubes in the pan. Place the pan on the hot plate. "What is happening? Is the ice melting, freezing, or boiling?" Remove the pan before the water boils. "Yes, it is melting because it is getting warm."

c. Place the pan back on the burner until the water begins to boil. "What is happening now? Is the water freezing, melting, or boiling? Yes, it's boiling. When water boils it turns into *(steam)*."

d. Pour the water from the pan into a metal cup. "Watch what I do." Place the cup in the freezer compartment of the refrigerator. "Now what will happen to the water? Will it boil, freeze, or melt?"

6. Arrange the following on a table at a distance from the group: an ice cube which is not melting, an ice cube which is at least half melted, a pan of boiling water on the hot plate. Working with each child in turn, ask:

a. "Point to the water that is melting."
b. "Point to the water that is frozen."
c. "Point to the water that is melting."
d. "Point to the water that is boiling."
e. "Point to the water that is frozen."

It is difficult for children to grasp this information in one lesson. Repeat the lesson or parts of it several times, emphasizing the words *boil, freeze, melt.* For variety, use juice, lemonade, and other liquids.

Lesson 4—*(Introductory)* Evaporation

Objective—To demonstrate an elementary understanding of evaporation

Materials—

Paper towel with the child's name written on it
Container or basin nearly full of water
Drying rack or line
Wet sponge
Chalkboard

Procedure—

1. Show the basin of water. "What is this?" Give each child a paper towel. "What will happen if we put our paper towels in the water?" Accept responses. Then have the children place their towels in the water to check their guesses. "What *did* happen? Were our guesses correct?"

2. "What will happen if we hang the towels up for awhile?" Place the towels on the drying rack. Accept guesses as to what will happen. Check the towels later. When they have dried, ask, "What *did* happen? Were our guesses correct?"

3. "What will happen if we put our hands in the water?" Have the children wet their hands. "What *did* happen? Were our guesses correct?"

4. "Now wave your hands around and shake them. What happened? Where do you suppose the water went?" Accept responses. Affirm or inform the children that the water went into the air. "Can we see the water in the air? No, we can't see it, but we know it is there."

5. "There is a special word to tell what happens when water goes into the air. The word is *evaporation.* The water evaporates—it goes into the air." Have the children repeat the word.

6. Have the children wet their hands again. "Are your hands wet or dry? Shake them. Now are they wet or dry? How did they dry? Where did the water go?" Remind the children that the water evaporated—it went into the air. Have them practice stating the explanation. "The water evaporated—it went into the air."

7. "Here is a wet sponge. I'll use it to wet the chalkboard. Watch what happens." Wet a portion of the chalkboard. It will begin to dry immediately. "What is happening to the water I put on the chalkboard? It is *evaporating,* isn't it?" Ask each child, in turn, "When water *evaporates,* where does it go?"

8. "Think for a minute about what happens when it rains. What happens to things outside when it rains? Yes, things get wet. Does everything stay wet after the rain stops? No, things get dry again. Where does the water go, as the things begin to dry? Right, into the air. When water goes into the air as things dry, we say the water is _(evaporating)._"

9. Repeat any of the above discussions or experiments if the children have difficulty with the terminology or the concept.

Shortly after this lesson is completed, present the lesson on clouds (Unit XI, Lesson 12).

Lesson 5—*(Introductory)*
Floating and Sinking

The concept of sinking and floating is a complex physical law having to do with the amount of water displaced by the object. Therefore, it is not essential, if indeed possible, for preschool children to understand the true principles of floating and sinking. Rather, what is intended here is that the children become familiar with the terms *float* and *sink* in relation to simple observations. The children should be given further opportunities to experiment with objects and water and to use these words in directed play or in additional lessons.

Do not teach that "light things float" and "heavy things sink" because the law governing whether an object floats or sinks is more complex than the meaning conveyed by the light/heavy association. Light and heavy are relative terms; nothing is light or heavy except in comparison to another object—a relationship difficult for the preschool child to comprehend. (For instance, the question of why a penny—which feels relatively light—sinks instead of floats requires an explanation that is beyond the child's ability to cope.) Although the light/heavy explanation may appear to provide the child with an elementary understanding of why things float or sink, the explanation creates more problems than it solves. It misinforms the child and teaches something that will have to be unlearned later.

Objective—To state whether an object placed in water floats or sinks

Materials—

Water table or tub filled with water

Smocks or aprons (optional)

Six objects (including a toothpick) that will float in water

Six objects (including a rock) that will sink in water

Five additional objects, three that will float and two that will sink

Box to hold the objects

Procedure—

1. Show the filled water table or tub of water. "What is this?" Have the children put on smocks or aprons. "I have a box of things we're going to put in the water. Watch closely so you can tell me what happens. I'll put the first thing in the water. Then each of you will have a turn."

2. Show a rock. "What is this?" Drop the rock in the water. "What happened? Yes, the rock went to the bottom. When we put something in water and it goes under the water like the rock did, we say it *sank*." Remove the rock from the water. Drop it in again. "What happened to the rock? Yes, it sank." Remove the rock and set it aside.

3. Show the toothpick. "Not all things sink when we put them in water." Hand a child the toothpick. "What is this? Put it in the water and let's see what happens." Have the child drop the toothpick into the water. "What happened? Did it sink? No, it stayed on top of the water. When something stays on top of the water like the toothpick did, we say it *floated*." Remove the

toothpick. Drop it in again. "What happened to the toothpick? Yes, it floated." Remove the toothpick and set it aside.

4. Test the remaining objects: Show the object. "What is this?" Give a child the object, and ask the child to drop it in the water. "What happened?" *(It sank—it went under the water;* or, *It floated—it stayed on top of the water.)* Remove the object. Drop the object into the water a second time. "What happened?" Have the children repeat the answer. Remove the object and set it aside.

5. When all objects have been tested, review.

   a. "When we put something in the water and it goes under the water, we say it *(sank)*."

   b. "When we put something in the water and it stays on top of the water, we say it *(floated)*."

   c. Quickly drop three or four objects into the water, one at a time. For each object, ask, "What happened?"

6. Using five objects different from those used in the lesson, give each child a turn to observe what happens when an object is dropped in the water. "Kathy, this time I want you to tell us what happens when I put this in water." Caution the other children not to say anything. Drop the object in the water and ask, "What happened?" (If the child responds, "Goes to the bottom" or "Stays on top," say, "Yes, but did it *float* or *sink*?")

Lesson 6—(Reinforcement) Sorting Floaters and Sinkers

Before beginning this lesson, review note on page 35.

Objective—To sort four objects according to whether they sank or floated when placed in water

Materials—

Water table or tub filled with water

Smocks or aprons (optional)

Box with six objects that float and six objects that sink (These may be same objects used in Lesson 5)

Two additional boxes

Picture-Labels for FLOAT and SINK
   (See preparation instructions below)

Scissors

Blue marking pen

Glue

Preparing the materials—Reproduce the picture-labels (page 41). Cut them out. Color the water area blue. Paste each label on the side of a box.

Procedure—

1. Have the children put on their smocks or aprons.

2. "Yesterday we talked about what happened when we put these things" (indicate the 12 objects) "in this tub of water. Who remembers what happened? Some of the objects *(floated)* and some of the objects *(sank)*. Today we'll sort the objects according to whether they float or sink. We'll put all the things that float in this box and all the things that sink in this box." Show the two boxes and discuss their picture-labels.

3. Have the children take turns testing the objects. The child selects an object and places it in the water, states whether the object sank or floated, and decides in which box to place the object. (Point out the picture clues on the boxes, if necessary.)

4. When the 12 objects have been sorted, review. Point to the FLOAT box. "Why did we put all these things together?" Point to the SINK box. "Why did we put all these things together?"

5. Give each child a turn to sort four items according to whether they float or sink. Hand the child the objects and the two empty boxes. "Here are four things. Place them one at a time in the water. If the object sinks, put it in this box." (Indicate) "If it floats, put it in this box." (Indicate) "Work by yourself and sort these four things." Observe but do not assist the child other than to mention, if necessary, "You are to put all the things that float in one box and all the things that sink in the other box."

Lesson 7—(Reinforcement)
Solids, Liquids, and Gases

Objective—To distinguish among a solid, a liquid, and a gas

Materials—

Ice cube	Hot plate
Water in a glass	Hand puppet
Empty glass	Glass of lemonade
Pan containing	Lollipop
½ cup water	

Procedure—

1. "The other day we talked about how water can change forms. Water can become an ice cube or steam. Water can be frozen, it can be melted, it can be boiled. Today we'll learn some new words that tell what form the water is in."

2. "Let's look at this ice cube first. When water is in this form, we say it is a *solid*." Have the children repeat the word several times. "When water is in its solid form, we can hold it in our hands and we can feel its shape." Pass the ice cube around so each child can hold it. As it is passed around, ask, "What form is that water in?"

3. Show a glass of water. "Look at this water. When water is in this form, we say it is a *liquid*." Have the children repeat the word several times. "When water is in its liquid form, we can't feel its shape. If we took it out of the glass, we wouldn't be able to hold it. It would run all over. When water is in its liquid form, we can *pour* it." Demonstrate. Give each child a turn to pour the water from one glass to the other. As they do so, ask each, "What form is that water in?"

4. "Look at this water—and watch." Turn on the hot plate and direct the children's attention to the pan of water. When steam appears, ask "Do you remember what we call this? Yes, steam. When water is in the form of steam, we say it is a *gas*." Have the children repeat the word several times. "Can we hold water as a gas in our hands, like we did water as a solid—the ice cube? No. Can we pour water as a gas, like we did when it was liquid? No." Point to the steam and ask each child, "What form is this water in?"

5. With the three forms of water on the table, review:

   a. Point to the ice cube. "Water in this form is a *(solid)*."

   b. Point to the water in the glass. "Water in this form is a *(liquid)*."

   c. Point to the steam. "Water in this form is a *(gas)*."

6. Introduce the hand puppet and let the children talk to it freely for a while. Then have the puppet look at the three forms of water on the table and ask, "What's all this? Would you tell me what these different things are?" Ask the children to point as you name the various forms:

   a. "Point to the water that is a liquid."

   b. "Point to the water that is a gas."

   c. "Point to the water that is a liquid."

   d. "Point to the water that is a solid."

   e. "Point to the water that is a solid."

   f. "Point to the water that is a gas."

7. Using the puppet, work individually with each child apart from the group. "Today we learned about three forms of water. We learned water can be a solid, a liquid, or a gas. Other things can have solid, liquid, and gas forms also. Look at these." Show the child a glass of lemonade and a lollipop. "One of these is a solid and one is a liquid. Give the puppet the treat that is a solid." Have the puppet pretend to eat the lollipop. "Now give the puppet the treat that is a liquid." Pretend to have the puppet drink the lemonade.

Lesson 8—(Extension)
Changing Forms of Water

Objective—To explain how forms of water can be changed

Materials—

Ice cubes
Glass of water
Hot plate
Empty pan
Pan containing one cup of water
Refrigerator or freezer

Procedure—

1. Place an ice cube, a glass of water, and the hot plate with the pan of water on the table. "Yesterday we talked about the three forms water can have. It can be a *(solid)* like this ice cube. It can be a *(liquid)* like this glass of water. Or it can be *(gas)* like this steam. Today we'll talk about how a solid can be changed into a liquid, and a liquid into a gas." Remove all the objects from the table except the hot plate.

2. Place two ice cubes in the empty pan. "What form is this water in? *(solid)* If we put it on the stove and heat it, it will change forms. Watch." Heat the ice just until melted. "What happened? Right, the ice melted. The water changed forms. The water was a solid—now it is a *(liquid).*"

3. "We'll heat the liquid water and the water will change forms again. Watch." Heat until steam is evident. Point to the steam. "What is happening? The water is boiling and the water is changing forms. It was a liquid—now it is changing into a *(gas).*"

4. Review. "If we want to change solid water into liquid water, what do we do?" Be sure the children understand that the solid water must be *heated;* it must *melt.* "If we want to change liquid water into a gas, what do we do?" Be sure the children understand that the liquid water must be heated until it boils. Conclude. "We need heat to melt water (ice) and we need heat to boil water."

5. "What if we want to change liquid water into solid water (ice)? What do you suppose we can do? If we heat it, what will happen? Yes, it will turn to gas." If the children cannot answer, explain that liquid water must be frozen to turn it into a solid. Place a cup of water in the freezer and check it later or the next day.

6. Review.

   a. Hold up an ice cube. "What form of water is this? How can I change it to a liquid?"
   b. Hold up water in a glass. "What form of water is this? How can I change it to a gas?"
   c. Hold up water in a glass. "What form of water is this? How can I change it to a solid?"
   d. Hold up an ice cube. "What form of water is this? How can I change it to a gas?"

Continue to ask the same questions in varied order, until children can answer easily.

The concept of changing forms in Lessons 7 and 8 can be reinforced and extended with materials other than water. The children can be shown that butter may be melted or milk frozen. They should become aware that there are materials (rocks, for example) which do not change form under usual conditions. At least two or three additional lessons are suggested, since the vocabulary and concepts are difficult for preschool children. Using this vocabulary with things other than water will help the children to understand the concept more fully and to generalize.

Lesson 9—(Extension)
Using Water-Related Objects

Objective—To demonstrate through pantomime how a pictured water-related item would be used

Materials—Motor-Encoding Pictures (See preparation instructions below)

Preparing the materials—Reproduce the pictures (pages 42-47). Mount them on construction paper or cardboard.

Procedure—

1. "We do a lot of talking at school. Talking is a good way to tell people things, but there is another way, too. We can use our hands, our faces, and our bodies to act out things. That's what we're going to do today."

2. "I'll show you a picture having to do with a way we use water. You show us *how* to use the things in the picture."

3. Select a child to act out the first picture. Show the picture to the class.

   a. Instruct the child, "*Show* us what you would do with this." Accept the child's attempt, however limited. Remind the child to *show*, not *tell*.

   b. Discuss the picture in detail and the procedure which was used to "act it out." Suggest several appropriate alternative actions or a series of actions. For example, for Picture #1: "Here is a sink and a dishcloth and some dirty dishes. If we wanted to wash the dishes, what would we do first? *(Turn on the water.)* Then what? *(Put the dishes in the water.)* Then what? *(Add soap.)* Then what? *(Wash the dishes.)* Then what? *(Rinse the dishes.)*" Help the children decide on suitable motions for each step.

   c. Have all the children participate in the actions as you review and act out the sequence.

4. Use the remaining pictures in the same way, giving each child a turn.

5. If the children are enjoying the lesson and time permits, use the pictures a second time to play a guessing game. Show a picture to only one child. Ask the child to act out the picture without saying anything. The other children are to guess what the child is doing and which picture is being acted out.

Lesson 10—(Extension)
Water Animals

Objective—To identify partially hidden ocean animals in a picture

Materials—

Large underwater scene of ocean (See preparation instructions below)

Pictures of water animals in ocean settings (See preparation instructions below)

Individual pictures of a whale, an octopus, and a starfish (See preparation instructions below)

Ocean Worksheets #1, 2, 3 (See preparation instructions below)

Glue

Construction paper

Crayon or pencil for each child

Preparing the materials—

1. Reproduce the underwater scene (page 48), pictures of water animals in ocean settings (pages 49-51), and the individual pictures of the whale, octopus, and starfish (pages 52-54). Mount them on construction paper.

2. Reproduce Ocean Worksheets #1, #2, and #3 (pages 55-57). Make a copy for each child and extra copies for demonstration.

Procedure—

1. "Do we live in water or in air? Yes, people live in air. We *use* water for a lot of things, but we don't live in water. There are some animals that do live in the water. Today we'll talk about a few of them.

2. "The animals I'll show you live in the ocean. The ocean has lots and lots of water. It's bigger than this room or this school. It's bigger than a river or a lake."

3. Show the underwater scene. "Here is a picture of just a small part of the ocean." Point out and discuss features in the picture—the water and its color, the plants, the animals.

4. Show the pictures of the octopus, whale, and starfish in ocean settings. "These are three animals that live in the ocean."

   a. Show the octopus. "This is an octopus." Have the children repeat the word. "It has eight arms and lives in the ocean." Ask the children to describe other features which may be visible in the picture.

   b. Show the whale. "This is a whale." Have the children repeat the word. "It is very, very large. It also lives in the ocean and swims around in the water." Ask the children to describe other features apparent in the picture.

   c. Show the starfish. "This is a starfish." Have the children repeat the word. "It's easy to remember its name because it looks like a star." Trace the outline of the starfish to emphasize that shape. "Starfish also live in the ocean." Ask the children to describe other features apparent in the picture.

5. "Here are pictures of the same three animals. Can you remember their names?" Use the individual pictures of the starfish, whale, and octo-

pus. Hold them up, one by one in this order, and ask the children to name them: starfish, whale, octopus, octopus, whale, starfish, whale, starfish, octopus, whale, octopus, starfish, whale.

6. Place Ocean Worksheet #1 (five octopuses) on the table next to the picture of an octopus. Point to the worksheet. "There are lots of octopuses in this picture. Let's see how many we can find. Some are partly hidden, so we'll have to look closely. If you see one, tell us and then put your finger on it so we can all see it." Work with the children as a group to find and mark the five octopuses. Review by pointing to each one.

7. Give each child a copy of Worksheet #1. Have the children mark the five octopuses with crayons. Give help as needed. Collect all papers.

8. Show Ocean Worksheet #2 (five starfish) and the picture of a starfish. "On this paper, we'll look for all the starfish. I'll give each of you a paper. See how many starfish you can find. Remember, some of them are hidden, so look closely!" Give each child a paper. Assist the children as needed until all starfish have been found.

9. Show Ocean Worksheet #3 (five whales) and the picture of a whale. "On this paper, we'll look for all the whales. I'll give each of you a paper. See how many whales you can find. Remember, some of them are hidden, so look closely. This time I won't help you. I want you to see how many you can find all by yourself. Tell me when you think you have found all the whales."

Picture-Labels for FLOAT and SINK

Motor-Encoding Picture #2

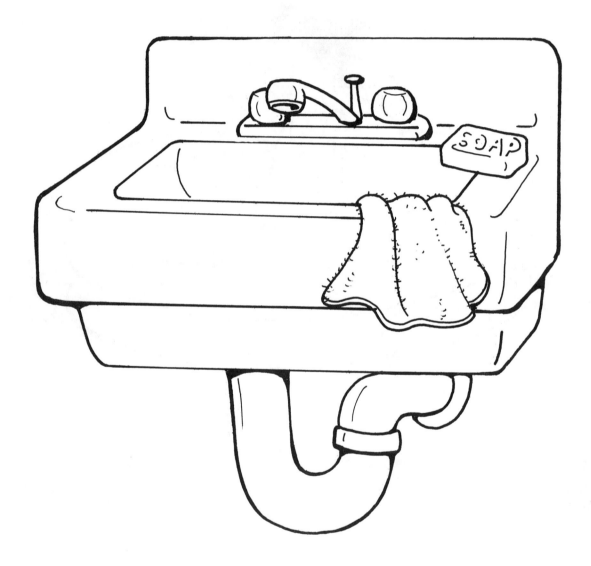

Underwater Scene

48

Water Animals

Water Animals

Water Animals

Whale

Octopus

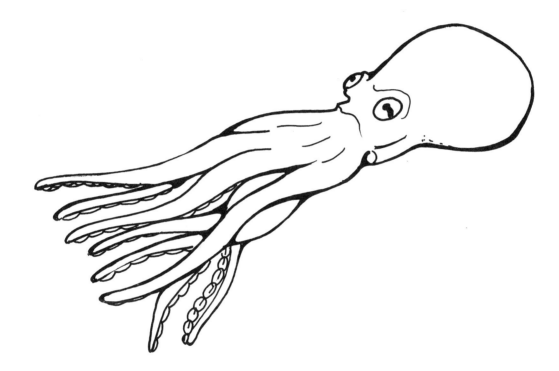

Starfish

Ocean Worksheet #1

Ocean Worksheet #2

Ocean Worksheet #3

Unit IV

Sound

Language Development—Goals, Objectives, and Vocabulary

Goals

To develop an understanding of the relationships among the ear, sound, and hearing

To associate sounds with their source and to classify these sounds according to a set of given attributes

Objectives

Receptive

The student will:

1. Comprehend the concept of sound traveling through the ear to the brain

2. Be aware of the presence of sound

3. Associate the relationship of proximity to the sound source with ability to hear

4. Be aware of the relationship of obstruction of the ear to hearing and not hearing

5. Be aware that sound must be able to get into the ear through the opening in the ear to be heard

6. Be aware of the articulators and their significance in making sounds and words

7. Comprehend the significance of each articulator in forming words

8. Comprehend the concept of vibrations and associate vibrations to sound making

9. Classify objects that vibrate and cause sound

10. Follow a series of directions involving identification, labeling, and categorizing three types of musical instruments

11. Associate and match homemade instruments to commercial instruments

12. Discriminate between loud/soft and high/low sounds

13. Follow directions incorporating high/low and soft/loud sounds

14. Match objects to their appropriate sounds

Expressive

The student will:

1. Label three musical instruments

2. Contrast the similarities and the differences in the production of sound made by three instruments

3. Label common objects as one of three types of musical instruments

4. Label sounds as loud or soft

Vocabulary

close	vibrations	drum	musical instruments
hearing	guitar	banjo	quietly
throat	triangle	horn	loudly
tongue	vocal cords	music	softly
lips	travel	percussion	high
teeth	through	wind	low
vibrate		string	

Lesson 1—*(Introductory)* Hearing

Objective—To demonstrate an understanding of the relationship between ability to hear and covered or uncovered ears

Materials—

Hearing picture set
  (See preparation instructions below)

Picture of The Outer Ear
  (See preparation instructions below)

Dial-type wristwatch

Record and record player

Preparing the materials—

1. Reproduce the picture of the outer ear (page 69). Mount it on construction paper.

2. Reproduce the Hearing Picture Set (page 70). Cut apart the four pictures and mount each on construction paper.

Procedure—

1. Present the picture of the outer ear. "What is this? Yes, it is an ear. What do we use our ears for? Right, for hearing. And what do we hear with our ears? Yes, sounds from all around us come into our ears, and we hear them. The sound goes into our ears through this opening" (show on the drawing), "and then it travels to our brain. It is our brain that tells us what the sound is. How do you know whether the sound you hear is a car horn or someone talking? Your brain tells you."

2. Hold the wristwatch a few feet in front of one child. "Can you hear the ticking of this watch?"

(No.) Hold the watch next to one ear. "Can you hear it now? Yes, you can hear it because it is close to your ear." Conclude. "Whether or not we can hear a sound depends on how loud the sound is, and how close it is."

3. Have the child cover one ear. Hold the watch next to the covered ear. "Can you hear the watch now? Why not?" *(The opening to the ear is closed by the hand, which keeps the sound from traveling into the ear.)* Put the watch next to the child's other ear. "Can you hear it now? Why can you hear it with this ear and not the other ear?" *(This ear has no hand covering it, so the sound is able to get in.)* Repeat the experiment quickly with each child. Conclude. "In order to hear, the sound must be able to get into the ear through the opening. If anything is over the opening, we cannot hear the sound."

4. "How many ears do you have? Where are they? Touch your ears. Why do you suppose you have two ears? *Two* ears help you hear sounds all around you. Let's do an experiment to find out how our ears work."

5. "Put your hands over your ears." Play the record. "Can you hear the record?" The children should be able to hear it. "Take your hands off your ears. Can you hear better with your hands over your ears or with your hands *not* over your ears?" Play the record again and have the children alternately cover and uncover their ears. Ask the question again. "Can you hear better when your ears are covered or uncovered? Why can you hear better when your ears are uncovered? *(The sound can get into the ears because nothing is in the way.)* Why do you have trouble hearing when your

ears are covered?" *(The sound has trouble getting in, because our hands are in front of the ear openings.)* Conclude. "We hear better when our ears are uncovered, because the sound can get into our ears."

6. "This time let's see if we can hear better with one ear or with both ears."

   a. Have the children cover and uncover their right ears as the record is played. "Can you hear better with one ear or with both ears uncovered? Why?" *(With one ear covered, the sound can't get into that ear easily; then we are mostly hearing with only one ear.)*

   b. Have the children cover and uncover their left ears as the record is played. "Can you

hear better with one ear or with both ears uncovered? Why?"

   c. Conclude. "We hear better with two ears than with one ear."

7. Show each child, in turn, two pictures from the Hearing Picture Set according to the following combinations:

   a. Child 1: Pictures 1 and 3
   b. Child 2: Pictures 2 and 4
   c. Child 3: Pictures 1 and 4
   d. Child 4: Pictures 2 and 3
   e. Child 5: Pictures 1 and 2

As each pair of pictures is shown, ask the child, "If I played the record again, point to the child who would be able to hear it better."

Lesson 2—*(Introductory)* Making Vocal Sounds

Objective—To state whether it is possible to make a sound under certain conditions

Materials—

Hand mirrors—one for each child (or large mirror that several children can look in together)

Procedure—

1. "We found out that we needed our ears to hear sounds and that we could hear better with two ears than with just one. Today we'll talk about how we can *make* sounds. What kind of sound am I making right now? Right, I am talking, and talking is a sound. But we need more than our mouths to talk. If we just move our mouths, we aren't talking." Demonstrate moving your mouth in silence, and have the children do the same. "There are other parts of our bodies we use with our mouths when we talk."

2. "When we talk or sing or whisper, the sound comes from our throats." Have the children place their hands on their throats and talk. "Can you *feel* the sound?" Give each child a hand mirror. "Look in the mirror and talk. You can see your throat moving."

3. "We can make all kinds of sounds with our throats." (Hum, laugh, but do not talk.) "But if we want to talk and have people understand us, we need to use our lips" (point to your lips) "and our tongues" (point to your tongue) "and our teeth." (point to your teeth)

4. Have the children look in the mirror again.

   a. "Close your mouth. Look in the mirror. Make sure your lips stay together. Now try to say your name. Try to talk. Can you talk without moving your lips? Can you hum without moving your lips? Yes, you can hum and make a sound, but you can't make *words* without moving your lips. Lips help us form words."

   b. "Open your lips, but put your teeth together as if you've just taken a big bite of a sandwich." (Demonstrate) "Look in the mirror. Make sure your teeth stay together. Now try to say your name. Try to talk. Can you talk with your teeth together? Can you hum with your teeth together? Yes, you can hum and make a sound, but you can't make *words* without moving your teeth. Teeth help us form words."

   c. "Hold your tongue between your fingers." (Demonstrate.) "Look in the mirror. Keep holding your tongue. Don't let it move. Try to say your name. Try to talk. Can you talk without moving your tongue? Can you hum without moving your tongue? Yes, you can hum and make a sound that comes from your throat, but you can't make *words* without moving your tongue. Our tongues help us form words."

    d. Review. "In order to talk, what do we need? Yes, our tongues, lips, teeth, and all the things in our throats that we can't see."

5. Give each child a turn to act as the "model" and a turn to answer the following questions:

    a. Tell Child 1: "Close your lips and don't open them." Ask Child 5: "Will _____ be able to say his name? Why not?" *(He needs his lips to form words.)*

    b. Tell Child 2: "Hold your tongue with your fingers." Ask Child 3: "Will _____ be able to hum? Why?" *(The hum sound comes from the throat. The child doesn't need the tongue to hum.)*

    c. Tell Child 3: "Hold your tongue with your fingers." Ask Child 4: "Will _____ be able to say his name? Why not? *(He needs his tongue to form words.)*

    d. Tell Child 4: "Put your hands over your ears." Ask Child 1: "Will _____ be able to say her name? Why?" *(Even if her ears are covered, she can speak.)*

    e. Tell Child 5: "Close your lips and don't open them." Ask Child 2: "Will _____ be able to hum? Why?" *(The hum sound comes from the throat. He doesn't need his lips to hum.)*

There are acceptable answers other than those suggested. The important aspect of the answer is whether or not the child indicates understanding of the relevancy of the tongue and lips in forming words.

Lesson 3—(Introductory)
Sound Vibrations

Objective—To demonstrate understanding that vibrations cause sound

Materials—

    Musical triangle and its striker

    Shallow pan or dish containing water

    Thin 12-inch ruler

    Rubber band stretched over a cut milk carton (See preparation instructions below)

    Radio or piano

Preparing the materials—Cut the top from a half-gallon milk carton so that the remaining bottom section is 2″ deep. Stretch a ¼″ thick rubber band around the carton and over the opening.

Procedure—

1. Present the triangle. Strike it to make it vibrate. Have the children listen to the sound. Touch the triangle to stop the vibration. Have the children listen again. They hear no sound. "What makes the sound of the triangle? When we strike the triangle, it vibrates, it moves. Can each of you say *vibrate*? The vibrations make the sound. The triangle is moving, even though you can't see it." Strike the triangle again, and give each child a turn to feel the vibrations by touching the triangle gently with a fingernail.

"There is another way to show that the triangle is really vibrating. Watch." Strike the triangle, then plunge it into the pan of water so the children may observe the waves made by the vibrations. "You can see that the triangle is vibrating because it makes the water move. The waves in the water are caused by the vibrations of the triangle."

2. "We heard the vibrations the triangle made, we felt them with our fingernails, and we saw the vibrations the triangle made in the water. Now we will do an experiment where we can not only hear the vibrations but see and feel them easily.

Listen to this sound." Make the ruler vibrate as shown in the diagram.

"Did you hear that sound? Did you see the vibrations of the ruler? Now I want each of you to make the ruler vibrate so you can hear the vibrations, see them, and feel them." Give each child a turn to do the experiment. "What is making the sound we hear? Yes, it's the vibrations, the movement of the ruler, that makes the sound. Do you see how the vibrations make the ruler move? Can you feel the vibrations of the ruler with the hand that holds the ruler on the table?"

3. "Let's try some other experiments to see if we can find out what causes sounds." Present the

rubber band stretched over the milk carton. "What do you think will happen if we make the rubber band vibrate? Listen." Pluck the rubber band.

"Who can tell us what happened? Yes, the vibrations made the sound. Whenever there is a sound, something is vibrating, something is moving."

4. Turn on the radio (or play the piano) and have the children touch it while it's being played. Then stop the sound. "What did you feel? Yes, *vibrations* made the sound."

5. Have the children hold their fingers against their throats and talk or hum. "What do you feel? Yes, vibrations. Your vocal cords are vibrating— they are moving. The vibrations make the sound you can hear and feel."

6. Allow time for the children to use the materials for further experiments with vibrations. As they work, discuss with them how the sounds are made by *vibrations*.

Lesson 4—(Reinforcement) Traveling Sound

Objective—To use a homemade telephone

Materials—

Empty soup can with one end removed—one for each child

Hammer and a nail

1″ two-holed button—one for each child

Pieces of wire, 10 feet long, fine enough to be threaded through the buttonholes—one piece for each pair of children

Procedure—

1. "We've talked about how we hear sounds and how we make sounds. Today we'll talk about how sounds can travel through things." Walk six or seven feet from the children. "Can you hear me? Do you know why? The sound is going from me to you *through* something. What is the sound going through to get to you? Yes, through the

air. The vibrations from the sounds I make when I talk go through the air, and you can hear me."

2. "Sounds can go through other things besides air. The vibrations can go through water and through wood, for instance." Instruct the children to put one ear directly on the table and cover the other ear. Tap the table with your finger. "Can you hear that sound? Yes, you can hear it because the vibrations can go through the wood."

3. "I'm going to go out in the hall and talk. Listen carefully and see if you can hear what I say." Leave the room and talk softly in the hall. Return. "Could you hear me? No, you couldn't. I was too far away, and the vibrations couldn't come all the way from there to here in the air."

4. "When we want to talk to someone who is far away—maybe even in another city—what do we use? Yes, a telephone. There are wires in the telephone, and the vibrations from our voices travel along the wires for a long way. Today we'll

make something like a telephone, so we can hear each other talking even when we aren't close together the way we are now."

5. Give each child a can; help the children to punch a small hole in the center of the bottom with the hammer and nail. Have each child select a partner, and give each pair of children a length of wire. Help each child in the pair to thread one end of the wire through the hole in the can from the outside to the inside. Then thread the wire up through one hole in the button and down through the other hole. Twist the end of the wire around the wire beneath the button to secure.

6. Have the children stand ten feet apart, preferably in different rooms. Have each child hold

one end of the tin-can telephone. Direct one child in each pair to place the can next to one ear like a telephone receiver. Direct the other child to hold the can close to the mouth like a telephone mouthpiece. Show the children how to use the cans to converse and listen and how to alternate the can from ear to mouth. Have them experiment to see if they can hear better by using the phones or by speaking to each other without the phones. They can whisper, sing, and talk. As the children experiment, talk about how their voice sounds travel along the wire between the two cans.

Lesson 5—(Reinforcement) Musical Instruments

Children must have some experience playing musical instruments before undertaking this lesson.

Objective—To identify percussion, wind, and string instruments

Materials—

A toy drum for each child
A toy horn for each child (labeled with the child's name) and one for demonstration
A toy banjo for each child
Record player
Recorded march music

Procedure—

1. Play the march record. "What did you hear? _(Music.)_ Were those voices that made the music? What did make the music? _(Musical instruments.)_ Do you know the names of any musical instruments?" Give the children time to offer the names of any instruments they might know.

2. Show a drum, banjo, and horn. "Here are three musical instruments. Each of these is played a different way. Today we'll talk about the three kinds of musical instruments. Some instruments you hit" (demonstrate with the drum) "to make

the sound." Let each child hit the drum. "Some instruments you blow into" (demonstrate with horn) "to make the sound." Let each child blow the horn. "With some instruments you pluck the strings" (demonstrate with the banjo) "to make the sound." Let each child pluck the strings.

3. Hold the drum. "Look at this instrument again. What is the name of this instrument? Yes, it's a drum. How do we play a drum? How do we make vibrations and sound with a drum? Yes, we hit it. Listen carefully, because I'm going to teach you a new word. When we hit an instrument to play it, it is called a _percussion_ instrument." Have the children repeat the word. "The drum is a percussion instrument. We hit it to play it. What kind of instrument is the drum? Why is it a percussion instrument?" Have the children pretend to play percussion instruments for awhile. Encourage them to make appropriate sound effects.

4. Hold the horn. "Look at this instrument. Is this a percussion instrument? No, it's not a percussion instrument because we don't hit it to play it. What is the name of this instrument? How do we make vibrations and sound with it? Yes, it is a horn, and we blow into it. When we blow into an instrument to play it, it is called a _wind_ instrument. We use air and wind from our bodies to play the instrument. The horn is a

wind instrument. We blow into it to play it. What kind of instrument is the horn? Why is it a wind instrument?" Let the children pretend to play wind instruments, including sound effects.

5. Hold the banjo. "Look at this instrument. Is this a percussion instrument? Do we hit it to play it? Is it a wind instrument? Do we blow into it to play it? What is the name of this instrument? How do we make vibrations and sound with it? Yes, it is a banjo, and we pluck on the strings. When we play an instrument by plucking on the strings, we call it a *string* instrument. The banjo is a string instrument. We pluck the strings to play it. What kind of instrument is the banjo? Why is it a string instrument?" Let the children pretend to play string instruments, using sound effects.

6. Review. "We've learned that there are three kinds of instruments. There are percussion instruments like this drum, string instruments like this banjo, and wind instruments like this horn." Place the three instruments in a row on the table. Have the children take turns following these directions:

   a. "Point to the percussion instrument. What is the name of that percussion instrument? Show how you play it."

   b. "Point to the wind instrument. What is the name of that wind instrument? Show how you play it."

   c. "Point to the string instrument. What is the name of that string instrument? Show how you play it."

   d. "Point to the wind instrument. What is the name of that wind instrument? Show how you play it."

   e. "Point to the percussion instrument. What is the name of that percussion instrument? Show how you play it."

7. "I'll play the record again, and you can play the instruments while you march to the music." Give each child a horn. "What is the name of that instrument? How do you play it? What kind of instrument is it?" Play the music and allow the children to march and play their horns. Collect the horns.

8. Give each child a drum. "What is the name of this instrument? How do you play it? What kind of instrument is it?" Play the music and allow the children to march and play their drums. Collect the drums.

9. Give each child a banjo. "What is the name of this instrument? How do you play it? What kind of instrument is it?" Play the music and allow the children to march and play their banjos. Collect the banjos.

Lesson 6—*(Extension)*
Matching Musical Instruments

Objective—To match a homemade instrument with a purchased instrument of the same type (percussion, wind, string)

Materials—

Cigar box
Three rubber bands, ¼″ thick
Six thumbtacks
Pop bottles—one for each child and one for the teacher
Paper drinking straws—one for each child and one for the teacher

Scissors
Empty 3-pound coffee can
3 large balloons
2 yards of string
Empty soup can with top lid removed
Can opener
Hammer
4″ nail
Recorded march music
Record player
Toy horn
Cymbals (or drum, if children are not familiar with cymbals)
Toy violin or other stringed instrument

Procedure—

1. "Who can remember the three kinds of instruments we talked about yesterday? How do we play percussion instruments? How do we play string instruments? How do we play wind instruments?"

2. "Today we'll make some instruments of our own. Then we'll play them and decide whether they are wind instruments, string instruments, or percussion instruments."

3. Help the children assemble the following instruments.

   String instrument: Cut the lid from the cigar box. Stretch three rubber bands across the opening of the box. Use thumbtacks on the side of the box to tighten the rubber bands.

   Wind instrument #1: Pop bottle (needs no alteration).

   Wind instrument #2: Partially flatten about half of one end of a drinking straw and cut off the corners, as shown in the diagram.

   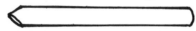

   Make one for each child and one for the teacher. Label each with the child's name.

   Percussion instrument #1: Remove the top and bottom from the coffee can. Cover one end with rubber from a slit balloon. Pull the rubber tightly over the edges of the can and tie it with string.

   Percussion instrument #2: Punch a hole with the hammer and nail through the bottom of the soup can. Insert a string through the hole and knot it. Place the nail beside the can.

4. Place these instruments in a row on the table. Only the teacher's drinking straw wind instrument should be displayed. "Now let's decide what kind of instrument each of these is. Watch how I play it, and then tell me if it is a percussion instrument, a wind instrument, or a string instrument." As you play each, ask, "How am I making sound with this? What kind of instrument is it?"

   a. String instrument: Pluck the rubber band strings as on a guitar or banjo.

   b. Wind instrument #1: Blow across the top of the bottle.

   c. Wind instrument #2: Blow into the flattened end of the straw. Optional: While blowing, cut off pieces of the other end of the straw one at a time. The pitch will rise as the horn gets shorter.

   d. Percussion instrument #1: Tap the end of the can covered by the balloon section as with a drum.

   e. Percussion instrument #2: Hold the can by the string and strike the side of the can with the nail.

5. Give each child one of the homemade instruments. Ask, "How are you going to play it? What kind of instrument is it?" Play the record and encourage the children to play along with their instruments.

6. Have the children trade instruments. Again ask each child, "How are you going to play the instrument? What kind of instrument is it?" Play the record and let the children play along again.

7. Have the children trade instruments a third time. Be certain that each child has a chance to play all three instruments. Place the toy horn, the cymbals (or the drum), and the violin on the table. Address each child in turn, "I have three instruments on the table. One is a percussion instrument. One is a wind instrument. One is a string instrument. You are holding an instrument, and you know how to play it. Point to which of these instruments you would play the same way as the instrument you are holding."

Lesson 7—(Extension)
Making Instruments

Objective—To demonstrate how a common object can be used as percussion, wind, or string instrument

Materials—

Several large rubber bands
Record player
Recording

Procedure—

1. "We've learned the three kinds of instruments. What are they? Yes, percussion, string, and wind. Today you'll get a chance to make your own instruments."

2. Ask one child to choose any object in the room and give it to you. Ask the children to label the object and describe what it is used for. "Now I am going to change this object. I am going to make it into a musical instrument." You might blow on the object in some way to create sound, stretch rubber bands around it to pluck, or tap it in some way. Ask the group to tell whether your homemade instrument is percussion, wind, or string.

3. Tell the children to walk around the room and search for objects that would make good instruments. Remind them that they can use rubber bands to turn an object into a string instrument.

4. After everyone has found an object, tell the children to sit in a circle and play their instruments all together. Play music for the children to accompany. Stop the music and ask only those with percussion instruments to play. If someone is not playing an object as a percussion instrument, suggest how the child might do so. Repeat the procedure for wind and string instruments.

5. Ask each child to play the instrument for the group. Have the children say whether it is a percussion, wind, or string instrument.

Lesson 8—(Extension)
Sound Variations

Objective—To identify loud and soft, high and low sounds

Procedure—

1. "We can make all kinds of sounds using our bodies and using objects. Today we are going to talk about different ways we make sounds." Knock loudly on the table. Knock quietly on the table. "I did the same thing both times—I knocked on the table. But the first time I knocked *loudly*" (demonstrate) "and the second time I knocked *quietly*" (demonstrate). Ask each child to knock loudly and then quietly. Ask each child in turn to knock two more times and to tell you whether each knock was loud or quiet.

2. Ask the children to stand up. "Let's all walk loudly." Stamp your feet. "Let's all walk quietly." Tiptoe as you walk. Have the children continue to walk. "Walk loudly . . . Walk quietly . . . Walk quietly . . . Walk loudly."

3. Discuss talking loudly (shouting) and talking quietly (whispering). Direct the children to say "Hello" loudly and quietly. Alternate these directions four or five times. Give each child a turn to say "Hello" loudly, then quietly, then quietly, then loudly.

4. "There is another way sounds differ. Listen." Say "Hello" in a high-pitched voice. Then say "Hello" in a low-pitched voice. "I said the same word both times, but one time I used a high voice and the other time I used a low voice. We can make high and low sounds, and we can make loud and quiet sounds." Have the children as a group repeat "Hello" with high voices and low voices.

5. Give each child a turn to follow these directions, but rotate the children rather than calling upon one child to complete the entire sequence consecutively.

   a. "Walk quietly."
   b. "Say 'Hello' in a high voice."
   c. "Say 'Hello' loudly."
   d. "Say 'Hello' in a low voice."
   e. "Walk loudly."
   f. "Say 'Hello' quietly."

Lesson 9—(Extension)
Sound Producers

Objective—To associate objects with their sounds

Materials—

Sound Pictures
(See preparation instructions below)

Sound tape
(See preparation instructions below)

Tape recorder

As many sound-producing objects as possible: a bell, newspaper to crush, musical instruments, spoons to strike together (See preparation instructions below)

Preparing the materials—

1. Reproduce the sound pictures (page 71). Mount on construction paper and cut them apart.

2. Record the following sounds on tape, allowing 10-second intervals between sounds:
   Hands clapping
   Vacuum cleaner running
   Whistle being blown
   Drum being played
   Water being poured into a glass
   Bell being rung
   Paper being ripped
   Voice saying "Hello, boys and girls!"
   Dog barking (or imitation of the sound)
   Piano being played
   Heavy footsteps
   Pencil being sharpened

3. Before the lesson, place the sound-producing objects around the room.

Procedure—

1. "Today we're going to make lots of sounds, and we're going to think about how they're made."

2. "First, think about the sounds you can make using parts of your body. When you think of a sound you can make with a part of your body, raise your hand and we'll all listen to the sound." Have the children take turns making sounds. Encourage the children to think of ways to use their hands, feet, and voices to make many different sounds: clapping, talking, singing, whistling, snapping fingers, stamping feet, humming, blowing noses.

3. "Very good! You thought of lots of sounds we can make with our bodies. Now look around the room. There are all kinds of things in the room that we can use to make sounds, too. Let's see how many different sounds we can make with things in the room." Have the children take turns making sounds with objects (any object they choose) in the room. You may need to demonstrate this activity before the children are able to respond freely.

4. Arrange the sound pictures in a row on the table so all are visible. Set up the tape recorder. "There are some sounds on the tape on this recorder. Each sound is different, and each sound was made by one of the things you see in these pictures." Discuss each picture briefly to be certain the children are familiar with the objects or actions shown. Play the sounds on the tape one at a time. After playing each sound, stop the recorder and ask the children to find the picture of the object or action that made the sound. Continue until the children have identified the pictures that correspond with the taped sounds.

The Outer Ear

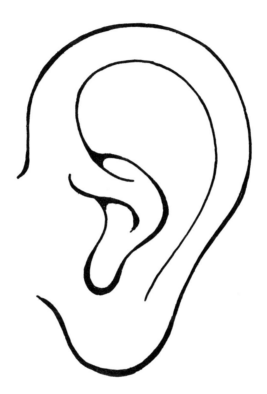

Hearing Picture Set

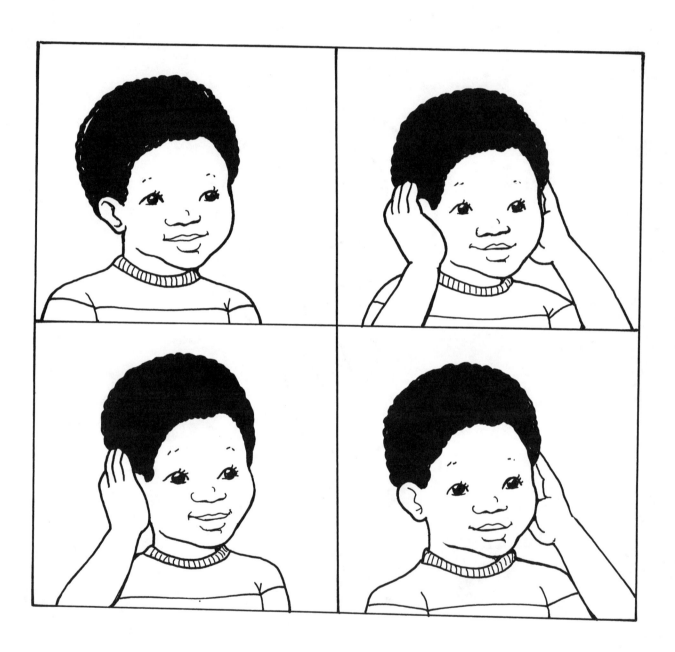

Sound Pictures

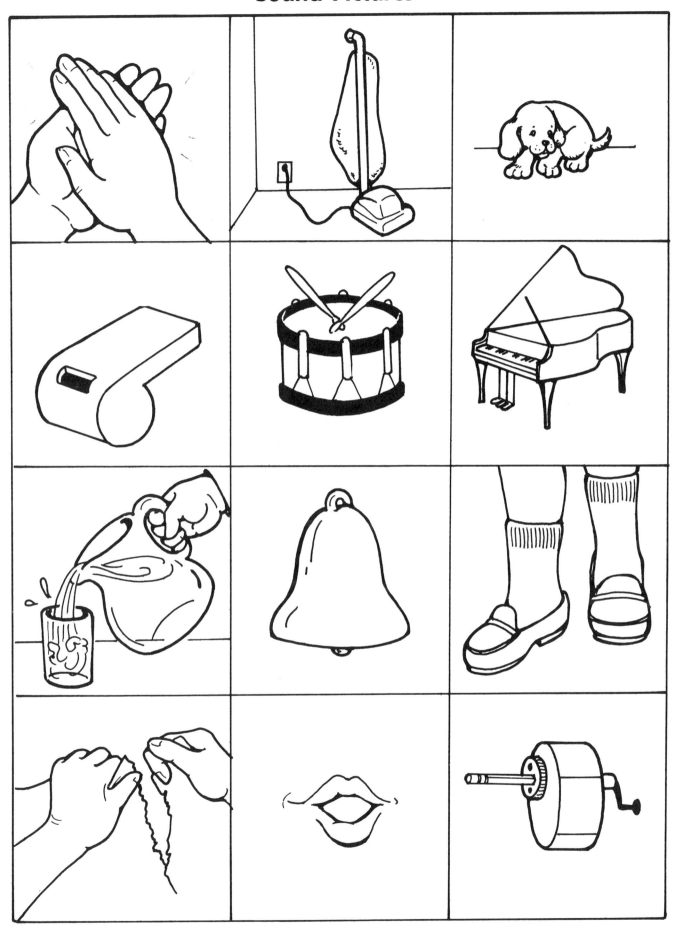

Unit V
Light

Language Development—
Goals, Objectives, and Vocabulary

Goals

To develop an understanding of the association of light with the sense of sight, related body parts, and other senses

To categorize attributes and functions of light

Objectives

Receptive

The student will:

1. Identify senses related to each body part

2. Comprehend the concept of light and dark

3. Classify actions done in light and in dark

4. Identify body parts associated with the eye (eyelid, eyelash, eyebrow, pupil)

5. Identify the action and function of various parts of the eye

6. Comprehend the meaning of artificial and natural light

7. Associate artificial light with various sources and attributes

8. Classify objects that are and are not sources of light

9. Associate the concept of light with the sense of sight

10. Associate the relationship between light and shadow

11. Recognize and match basic colors

Expressive

The student will:

1. Label body parts associated with the eye (eyebrow, eyelash, eyelid, pupil)

2. Contrast the similarities and differences of eyes

3. Label attributes and functions of the sun

4. Contrast the differences between natural and artificial light

5. Label basic colors

Vocabulary

light	artificial	electrical wires
dark	natural	plug
with	candle	cord
without	light bulb	shadow
day	flashlight	between
night	prism	inside
sun	batteries	half

Lesson 1—(Introductory)
Light and Dark

This lesson should be done in a room that can be darkened by turning off the lights. The room should have a door that can be shut, and there should be no windows (or the windows should be shaded).

Objective—To state activities one does in the light and in the dark

Materials—Chalk and chalkboard

Procedure—

1. Review the senses. "For what do we use our eyes? . . . For what do we use our ears? . . . For what do we use our hands? . . . For what do we use our noses? . . . For what do we use our tongues?"

2. "We know that we use all our senses to learn. We've already learned a lot about ourselves and about air and water by using our senses. For the next few days we'll be thinking mostly about just *one* of our senses—seeing. While you're in school or at home, think about how you're using your eyes."

3. "Can we see all the time? Can you see right now?" Darken the room. "Now can you see? Why not?" *(Because it is dark.)* Turn the lights on again. "Can you see now? Why? What is in the room now that wasn't here when we couldn't see?" Darken and lighten the room several times. Each time there is a change from dark to light or light to dark, ask "Is there light in the room? Can you see?" Conclude. "We need light in order for our eyes to see. If there is no light, we can't see."

4. "Think about some of the things you do when you have light and can see. Raise your hand and I'll write your ideas on the chalkboard, so we'll be able to remember them and talk about them later." Write the children's responses. (*Read books, play, eat, get dressed, draw pictures, . . .*) Read back the list. Briefly discuss each suggestion. "You thought of lots of things we do when we have light and can see. First, you said we could _____" (read the first item on the list) "when we have light. Could we _____ if there was no light?" Darken the room to help the children decide if they could engage in the activity without light. In some instances, such as eating, it would be possible but much more difficult to perform the activity without light. Through this process, help the children to realize that light lets us do many things; and without it we could not do some things at all.

5. "There are some things we can do without light. Think hard; and when you have an idea, raise your hand. I'll write your answers on the chalkboard." Write the children's responses. (*Sleep, listen to music, hear people talking, smell food cooking, . . .*) Read back the list. Briefly discuss each suggestion. "First, you said we could _____" (read the first item) "when we have no light. Can we _____ in the dark? Do we need our our eyes to _____? What sense *do* we use to _____?" Help the children to understand in this way that when there is no light they can use senses other than sight.

Lesson 2—(Introductory) Eyes

Objective—To identify the eyelashes, the pupil, and the eyebrow

Materials—

Picture of The Eye
(See preparation instructions below)
Construction paper
Hand mirrors—one for each child
Red, green, and blue crayons—one set for each child

Preparing the materials—

1. Reproduce The Eye (page 83). Make a copy for each child and one extra copy.

2. Mount the extra copy on construction paper to make a poster.

Procedure—

1. Hold up the eye poster. "What is this? Yes, it's an eye. Look at this picture of an eye very carefully. The eye has several parts. Today we'll learn the names of those parts."

2. Point to each part of the eye and label it for the children.

   a. Point to the eyebrow. "This part is called an eyebrow."

   b. Point to the eyelid. "This is called an eyelid."

   c. Point to the eyelashes. "These are the eyelashes."

   d. Point to the pupil. "This is called the pupil."

3. Point to and label these parts again. Have the children repeat the labels.

4. Give each child a hand mirror. Instruct the children to look at and point to the eye parts as you name them and point to them on the chart. Caution the children to be careful not to put their fingers in their eyes when pointing.

   a. "Look at your eyelashes in the mirror. Point to your eyelashes."

   b. "Look at your eyebrows in the mirror. Put your finger on one of your eyebrows."

   c. "Look at the pupil (the black part) of your eye in the mirror. Point to the pupil of your eye."

   d. "Look at your eyelid in the mirror. Put your finger on your eyelid."

   e. Help the children to notice other parts of their eyes—the colored sections and the white section. Have the children compare the color of their eyes with that of other children.

5. Discuss the similarities of eyes. "Do you all have eyes? . . . Do you all have eyelashes? . . . Do you all have pupils? . . . Do you all have eyebrows? . . . Do you all have eyelids?"

6. Discuss the functions and characteristics of eye parts.

   a. "Look at your eyelids again. What can your eyelids do? *(Move up and down, open and close.)* Yes, our eyelids can close to protect our eyes. We can close them to keep out light that is too bright. They can keep dirt or wind out of our eyes."

   b. "Look at your pupils. What can they do?" Help the children discover that the pupil and colored part move around and enable us to see things in different directions without having to move our heads. Explain that the pupil is where the light comes into the eye. If there is very little light, the pupil gets bigger to let in more light; if there is a lot of light, the pupil gets smaller because the eye doesn't need that much light. If light conditions in the room can be changed to provide enough contrast to cause changes in pupil size, the children may observe this change in their mirrors.

   c. "Look at your eyebrows. What can you do with your eyebrows?" Discuss how the movement of eyebrows can change our facial expressions and how they help to keep dust and dirt out of our eyes. Have the children feel their eyebrows and conclude that they are composed of many tiny hairs.

   d. "Look at your eyelashes. What do you think they do?" Point out that they are attached to eyelids and move with the eyelids. Let the children observe this movement in their mirrors. Explain that the eyelashes help keep dirt and dust out of the eyes. Have the children close their eyes and feel their eyelashes. Conclude that they are also composed of tiny hairs.

7. Give each child a copy of the eye worksheet and three crayons. "Here is a picture of an eye. Find your red crayon. Mark the *eyelashes* on the picture. Find your green crayon. Mark the *pupil* on the picture. Find your blue crayon. Mark the *eyebrow* on the picture."

Lesson 3—*(Introductory)* Daytime and Nighttime

Teach this lesson on a bright, sunny day.

Objective—To differentiate daytime and nighttime scenes

Materials—

Picture of the sun
  (See preparation instructions below)

Pictures of daytime and nighttime scenes
  (See preparation instructions below)

Construction paper

Paste

Preparing the materials—Reproduce the picture of the sun (page 84) and the pictures of daytime and nighttime scenes (pages 85-87). Color the pictures and mount them on construction paper.

Procedure—

1. Begin by asking the following riddle: "I am big, round, and yellow. I live in the sky. I make light so everyone can see. Who am I? . . . Yes, the answer to the riddle is the sun. The sun gives us the light we need so we can see things. The sun is far, far away, but its light is so bright that it makes light for everything we do. It is so bright that we cannot look right at it without hurting our eyes. I have a picture of the sun here so everyone can see what it looks like." Show the picture and discuss the appearance and location of the sun.

2. "We've talked about the kinds of lights we can turn off and on, like the light in this room. The sun also gives us light. Can we turn the sun off and on? No!" Have the children go to the window and observe the light outside. "Can you see things outside? Is there light? Where is the light coming from? Does the sun shine all the time? What about when you're sleeping? When the sun is shining and it's light outside like now, it is day. When the sun isn't shining and it's dark outside, it is night."

3. Take the children for a walk outside. Emphasize the following points:

   a. Sunlight shows us the colors of things.
   b. Sunlight is warm. Have the children feel the temperature difference and note the light difference when standing in the sun and when standing in the shade.
   c. Sunlight helps plants grow.

4. Return to the classroom. "What are some of the things the sun's light does for us?" Help the children recall the discussion held during the walk.

5. "Is it day or night now? How do you know?" *(It's light outside; you can see the colors of things.)*

6. Show the pictures of daytime and nighttime scenes. Ask, "Is it day or night in this picture? . . . How do you know it is _____?" Discuss visual clues that indicate whether it is day or night. Discuss at least two visual clues for each picture.

Lesson 4—*(Introductory)*
Identifying Types of Light

Objective—To state whether a light has an artificial or a natural source

Materials—

Candle	Desk lamp
Matches	Flashlight

Procedure—

1. Review. "We've talked about day and night. In the day we get light from the *(sun)*. What do we use for light at night, when we don't have sunlight?" Discuss the children's answers.

2. Place the candle, the matches, the desk lamp, and the flashlight on the table. "Here are just some of the things we can use to make light at night."

   a. Light the match. Be sure the children know the word *match*. Discuss the difficulties in using a match as a source of light (the danger of fires, the flickering nature of the light, the weakness of the light, the brevity of the light). Darken the room so the children will experience the difficulties of trying to see with just the light from the match.

   b. Light the candle. Be sure the children know the word *candle*. Discuss the difficulties in using a candle as a source of light (the danger of fires, the weakness of the light, its flickering nature). Discuss its advantages over a match. (It is brighter, lasts longer, is safer.) Darken the room so the children will realize how different candle light is from sunlight or electric light.

   c. Remove the light bulb from the desk lamp and show it to the children. Be sure the children can identify it as a light bulb.

   Replace the bulb. Darken the room, leaving only the desk light burning. "This is another way we can have light at night. We can turn on lamps and lights around the house. And this is what we do, isn't it? We don't light candles because we have lamps and electricity. Lamps give us more light than candles can." Show the cord and plug and point out that electricity goes through wires to light the lamp.

   d. Show the flashlight. "What is this? Does it have a light bulb in it? Does it have wires? No, it doesn't have wires and we don't plug it in the way we do a lamp." Show the batteries. "These are called batteries. The batteries make the electricity to light up this little bulb, and the flashlight gives us light. Sometimes during storms, the electricity wires fall down and we use flashlights to see. Sometimes we use flashlights to find things in dark closets or outside at night." Darken the room and give each child a turn to use the flashlight to find an item or a child in the room.

3. "This kind of light—the kind that comes from candles, flashlights, and lamps—is called *artificial* light." Have the children repeat the word. "The light that comes from the sun is called *natural* light." Have the children repeat the word.

4. Take the children on a walk around the school and have them look for types of artificial light. "See how many different artificial lights you can find. Remember, artificial light is light that does *not* come from the sun." As the children locate lamps and ceiling lights (don't forget the light in the refrigerator), ask again whether the light is *natural* (from the sun) or *artificial* (not from the sun). Use these words as frequently as possible.

Lesson 5—*(Reinforcement)*
Differentiating Types of Light

Objective—To differentiate artificial and natural light

Materials—

Artificial Light Worksheet
  (See preparation instructions below)
Crayons—one for each child

Preparing the materials—Reproduce the Artificial Light Worksheet (pages 88-89). Make one 2-page worksheet for each child. Cut the worksheets into five strips as indicated.

Procedure—

1. "Yesterday we talked about natural light and artificial light. What is natural light? *(Light from the sun.)* What is artificial light?" *(Light not from the sun.)*

2. "We walked around the school and found many kinds of artificial light. Today we'll go outside and look for artificial lights. We know how we use artificial light in school and in our houses. Now we'll look for ways we use artificial light outside."

3. Take the children on a walk. Help them discover the many sources of artificial light outside (stoplights, car headlights and tail lights, porch lights, street lights, neon signs). Discuss the uses of each artificial light. Return to the classroom.

4. Present Strip #1.

   a. Give Strip #1 of the Artificial Light Worksheet to each child.

   b. "Look at the pictures on your paper. Three of the pictures show artificial lights. One of the pictures does not belong there because it is not an artificial light. Put your finger on the picture that does not belong." If the children have difficulty, explain that *book* does not belong because we don't get light from books.

   c. Give each child a crayon to mark the picture.

   d. Ask, "Why doesn't the picture of the book belong with the others?"

   e. Conclude. "The book does not belong *because* it is not an artificial light."

   f. Ask each child this question, in turn. Require the child to answer using the sentence form.

   g. Collect Strip #1.

5. Present the other strips one at a time in the same manner.

Lesson 6—*(Reinforcement)*
Sight and Light

This lesson should be done in a room that can be darkened.

Objective—To demonstrate an awareness that light is necessary for sight

Materials—

Five magazine pictures of familiar scenes
  (See preparation instructions below)
Construction paper
Scissors
Paste
Desk lamp

Preparing the materials—Cut out magazine pictures of familiar scenes. Mount each picture on construction paper.

Procedure—

1. Seat the children in the darkened room with only the desk lamp turned on. Hold up one of the pictures and ask, "Can you see this picture? Tell me about it." Turn the lamp off and hold up the second picture. "Can you see this picture? Can you tell me about it? Why not? What do we need in order to see the picture?" Turn the desk lamp on. "Can you see the picture now? We must have light to see." Briefly review Lessons 1 and 3 by asking what kind of light is being used in the room. "Does it come from the sun or from somewhere else?" Conclude. "It is not sunlight. We can turn it off and on."

2. Keep the lamp on. Hold up the third picture. "Can you see this picture? Tell me about it."

3. Keep the lamp on. "Now close your eyes." Hold up the fourth picture. "Remember, keep your eyes closed and tell me about the picture I am holding up. Can you tell me about it with your eyes closed? Now open your eyes. Tell me about the picture." Conclude. "Our eyes must be open in order to see. If our eyes are closed, the light cannot get into the pupils and we cannot see."

4. Review. "In order to see, we need two things. What are they?" *(Our eyes must be open; there must be light.)*

5. Present the pictures one at a time to each child.

   a. Turn the lamp off. Direct Child 1: "Keep your eyes open. Can you see the picture? Why not?" *(There is no light.)*

   b. Turn the lamp on. Direct Child 2: "Keep your eyes open. Can you see the picture? Why can you see it?" *(Eyes are open, light is on.)*

   c. Turn the lamp off. Direct Child 3: "Keep your eyes open. Can you see the picture? Why not?" *(There is no light.)*

   d. Turn the lamp on. Direct Child 4: "Keep your eyes open. Can you see the picture? Why?" *(Eyes are open, light is on.)*

   e. Turn the lamp off. Direct Child 5: "Keep your eyes open. Can you see the picture? Why not?" *(There is no light.)*

Lesson 7—*(Reinforcement)* Shadows

This lesson should be done in a room that can be darkened.

Objective—To demonstrate an awareness of the conditions necessary to make a shadow

Materials—

Gooseneck desk lamp with opaque shade

Box of familiar objects that can be identified from their shadows (scissors, bottle, spoon, fork, banana, paper square, circle, triangle, . . .)

Procedure—

1. Darken the room and turn on the gooseneck lamp. Focus the light on the wall. Put your hand between the light and the wall to cast a shadow of your hand. "What do you see on the wall? Yes, you see a hand. Is it a real hand? No, it's a *shadow* of my hand. I made the shadow by putting my hand between the light and the wall. My hand stops the light. The light cannot go through my hand, so there is a dark place on the wall where there is no light because my hand has stopped it. Do you suppose you could make a shadow?" Give each child a turn to make a shadow. Encourage the child to use the word *shadow.* Between turns, with the light shining on the wall, ask, "Why is there no shadow now? Right, there is nothing stopping the light. There has to be something between the light and the wall to make a shadow."

2. Have the children sit facing the wall on which the shadows are cast, with their backs to the light. They must be unable to see the objects that will be used to cast shadows. Bring out the box of objects. "I have some things here that I'm not going to show you. I'll make shadows with these things, and you decide what they are by looking at the shadows." Hold the objects one at a time in front of the lamp. Have the children name each object from its shadow. If the children are unable to identify an object, give them a clue. For each object, ask, "How do you know this is a _____? Yes, you can tell by the shape of the shadow." From time to time, show only the spot of light on the wall and ask, "Why is there no shadow now?" *(No object is blocking the light.)*

3. Have the children place their chairs so they can see the lamp, the table, and the objects. "We have seen shadows of several things. Now let's see if we can remember three things we need to make a shadow. We need a *light,* and *an object to make a shadow,* and the *wall where we see the shadow.* These things have to be in the right order to make a shadow. The object that makes the

shadow has to be *between* the light and the wall, like this." Demonstrate that there is no shadow if the object is placed behind or to the side of the light. Demonstrate that there is no shadow if the lamp is off.

4. "We're going to play Where's the Shadow? and I'm going to try to fool you." Set up one of the following situations for each child:

   a. The three elements are in the correct order, but the lamp is off.

   b. The lamp is on, but the object is behind the light.

   c. The lamp is on, but the object is to one side of the light.

Give each child a turn to explain why there is no shadow. Have the child remedy the situation and make a shadow.

Extension—

In subsequent lessons, provide additional experiences with shadows.

1. Help the children present a short shadow play using their hands, toy animals, or hand puppets to make animal shadows. Improvise simple stories. "Three little rabbits with furry ears were busy talking one day. They wanted to go somewhere. Finally they decided to go to the park to see the swans in the pond. They hopped over to the pond, and there they saw two beautiful swans swimming in the water. The rabbits got so excited! The swans looked so graceful and the water looked so cool! They wanted to go for a swim, too. So, in they jumped, but the water was get wet. They came out of the pond and shook and shook the water from their wet, droopy ears. And the swans, still swimming in the pond, just laughed and laughed."

2. Children generally enjoy experiences with their own shadows. Outdoors on a sunny day, help them to note their shadows made by sunlight (natural light). They can observe their own and others' shadows from different angles, try to run away from their shadows, and so on. Older children will enjoy playing shadow tag on the playground. A child is "tagged" when "IT" steps on that child's shadow.

3. Read Robert Louis Stevenson's poem, "My Shadow." The poem is particularly effective when read outdoors while the children are resting after a game of shadow tag or after observing shadows made by the sun. For younger children, use only the first stanza.

4. The shadow of a stationary object—a car parked for the day on the schoolyard, the flag pole, or even the school building itself—can be outlined by the children with string or chalk (if the shadow appears on asphalt or concrete). Later in the day, help the children to check changes in the shadow.

5. Have each child take a turn sitting sideways in front of the light, casting a shadow of the head on a piece of white paper taped to the wall. Trace the child's profile. Cut out this silhouette and mount it on black construction paper. These profiles make popular take-home papers.

Lesson 8—*(Extension)* Picture Boxes

Objective—To explain why one can or cannot see a picture under differing degrees of light

Materials—

Closure Shoebox
   (See preparation instructions below)
Flashlight
Magazine picture of an object
Index card
Closure Pictures
   (See preparation instructions below)

Preparing the materials—

1. Cover the box and lid of a shoebox separately with wrapping paper. Cut a 1" round "peephole" in the center of the lid. Cut a hole in one end of the shoebox large enough to insert a flashlight so the head of the flashlight is inside the box and the handle is outside (see diagram).

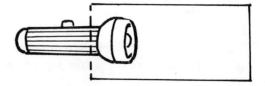

2. Cut out a magazine picture that will fit on the bottom of the box.

3. To make a set of Closure Pictures, collect simple pictures of familiar objects; cut each picture in half.

Procedure—

1. Place the magazine picture on the bottom of the box opposite the peephole. Present the closure shoebox without the flashlight. Place the index card over the flashlight hole. Have the children look through the hole in the lid. "Look inside. There is a picture in the box. Tell me about the picture." Have each child peek into the box through the hole in the lid and tell what is seen. *(It will be dark, and they will not be able to see the picture.)* Ask each child, "Why can't you tell me about the picture? Why can't you see it? Your eyes are open. What else do you need?"

2. Remove the index card. "Now there is light in the box. Can you see the picture? Why can't you see it very well?" *(The hole doesn't let in enough light to see the picture clearly.)*

3. Present the flashlight. "If we turn on the flashlight, do you think we'll be able to see inside the box? Let's try." Insert the flashlight and turn it on. Give each child a chance to look through the hole in the lid. "Now we have light in the box, and our eyes are open. Can you see the picture now?" Ask each child to tell about the picture after looking in the box. "We all could see the picture, couldn't we? Why couldn't we see it before?"

4. Using Closure Pictures, place half of each picture on the table. Place the other halves in your lap. One by one, place a half-picture from your lap in the shoebox. Give a child a turn to look into the box. "Look in the box and tell us what you see." Have the child describe what is seen. "The other half of the picture you see is on the table. Can you find it?" Place the two halves together to see if the choice was correct. Then return one half to the table and one to your lap.

5. Give each child a turn to look in the box and complete a picture.

Lesson 9—*(Extension)* Color Spectrums

Objective—To make a color spectrum

Materials—

Cardboard, large enough to cover one of the windows in the room

Scissors

Tape

Triangular prism

White tagboard, 3″ square

Small lump of clay

Colored magazine picture of a rainbow

Rainbow Colors Worksheet and construction paper triangles (See preparation instructions below)

Rainbow Colors chart (See preparation instructions below)

Paste

Preparing the materials—

1. Reproduce the Rainbow Colors Worksheet (page 90) on white paper. Make one copy for each child plus one extra.

2. Using violet, indigo, blue, green, yellow, orange, and red construction paper, reproduce the triangles (page 91). Cut them out. Assemble a set of seven triangles (one of each color) for each child plus one extra set.

3. Use the extra worksheet and set of triangles to make a Rainbow Colors chart, pasting the triangles on the pattern as shown below.

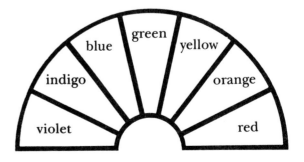

Preparing the room—Cut a horizontal slit about ⅛″ wide and 1″ long in the center of the cardboard that is to cover the window. Tape the cardboard to a window through which the sun is shining. Darken the other windows. Place a table near the window so the sun's rays fall on the table as they come through the slit in the cardboard. Set the prism lengthwise in the clay. Place the prism on the table so the sunlight passes through it and is projected on the wall opposite the window. Mount the white tagboard on the wall at that projection point so the spectrum appears on the tagboard. Mark the spot on the table where the prism must be to reproduce that spectrum. Remove the prism.

Procedure—

1. Discuss with the children what they have learned previously about light. *(It helps us see things; when it is blocked, it forms shadows.)*

2. "Today we are going to see something else that light can do." Point out the components of the experiment—the darkened room, the slit in the cardboard that allows light to enter, the white tagboard on the wall, the prism. Have the children practice saying the word *prism*.

3. "We think of the sun's light as white; and sometimes when we draw pictures, we color the sunlight yellow. But when the sun's light passes through this prism, we can see that the light of the sun is made up of many colors." Place the prism to show the spectrum on the tagboard. Explain how the sunlight comes through the prism and is reflected on the tagboard. Point

out that when we look at the sunlight through the slit in the cardboard it doesn't look as if it has any colors in it; but when we pass the light through the prism, we can see that there are seven colors in sunlight.

4. Point to and name the colors on the reflected spectrum—violet, indigo, blue, green, yellow, orange, and red. "Did you ever see these colors before? Have you ever seen a rainbow?" Allow the children to talk about rainbows. Show them the colored magazine picture of the rainbow. "Sometimes you can see a rainbow in the sky when it is raining and the sun is shining. The sunlight passes through the drops of rain the same way it passes through this prism and shows all the colors in the reflected spectrum and in the picture of the rainbow." Explain that these same colors always appear in the same order.

5. Show the Rainbow Colors chart. Point out the similarity between it and the spectrum made by the prism. "We are all going to make our own charts of the colors in sunlight." Give each child a Rainbow Colors Worksheet and a set of seven Rainbow Colors triangles. Point to the violet section on the assembled Rainbow Colors chart, and say to the children, "This is the first color you'll need. Everyone, pick up a violet triangle and paste it on your paper." Help the children to start at the left. Continue pasting until the seven triangles have been arranged to form the color spectrum. Children may need help in lining up the triangles to reproduce the semicircle of color shown on the Rainbow Colors chart.

The Eye

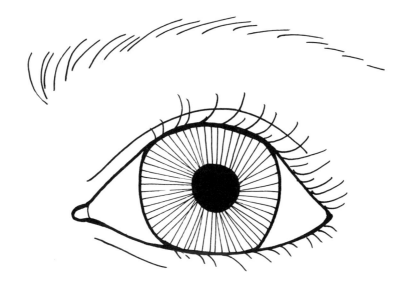

The Sun

Daytime and Nighttime Scenes

SUSAN B ANT
ELEMENTA

Daytime and Nighttime Scenes

Daytime and Nighttime Scenes

Artificial Light Worksheet

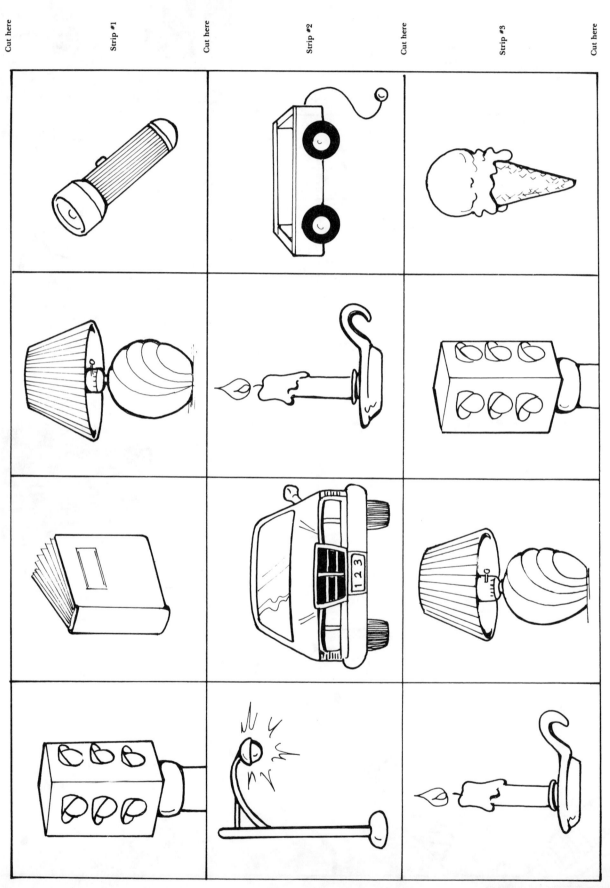

Artificial Light Worksheet (continued)

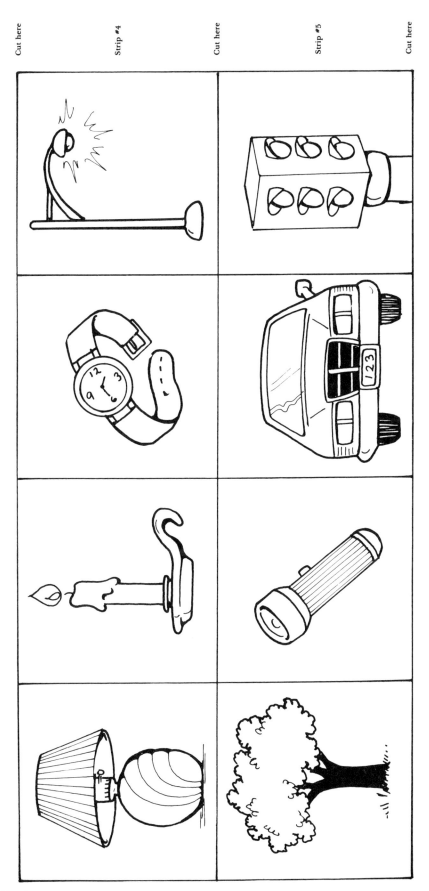

Rainbow Colors Worksheet

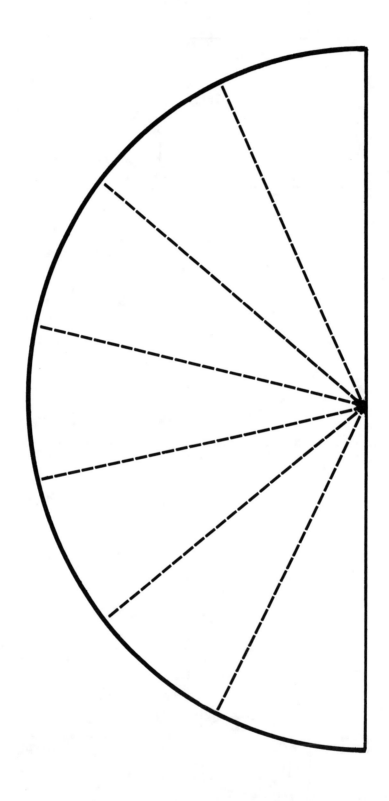

Triangles for Rainbow Colors Worksheet

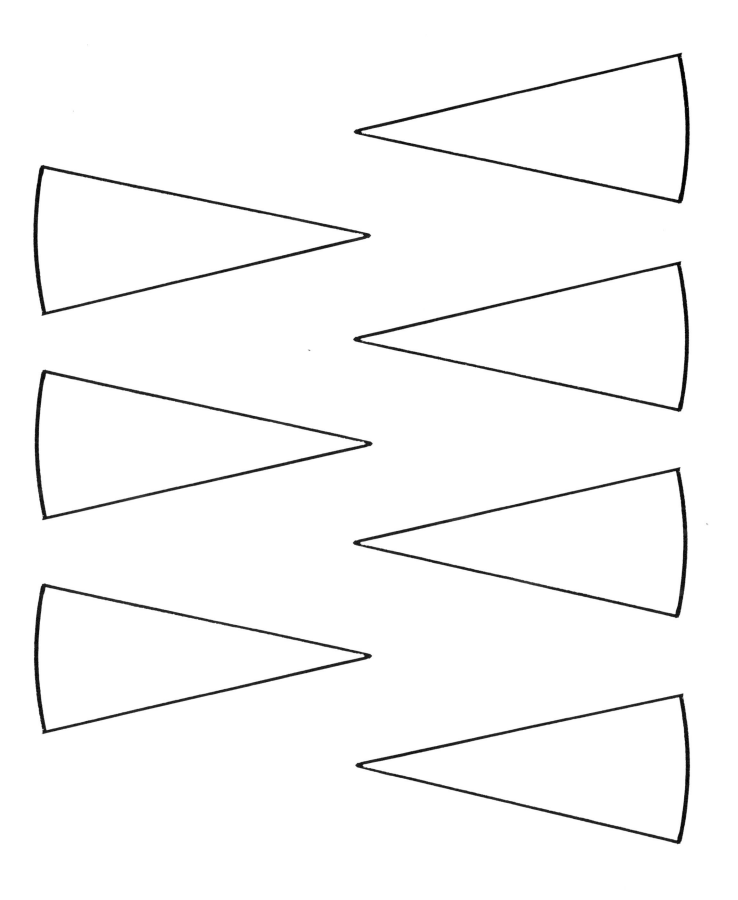

Unit VI
Living and Nonliving Things

This unit teaches the child that there are three types of living things—plants, animals, and people. Living things generally are divided into only two categories—plants and animals. However, it is difficult to teach the preschool child that people and animals belong to the same category; and for the child just beginning to understand classification, such precision seems unwarranted.

Language Development—Goals, Objectives, and Vocabulary

Goals

To demonstrate an awareness of the differences in the concepts *living* and *nonliving*

To categorize objects as living and nonliving, using a given set of characteristics

Objectives

Receptive

The student will:

1. Comprehend the concepts of *living* and *nonliving*

2. Classify objects as living and nonliving

3. Classify animals, plants, and people as living things

4. Identify objects as living and nonliving when given a statement that includes an embedded exclusionary form (*not*)

Expressive

The student will:

1. Express characteristics of living things to include eating, drinking, breathing, growing

2. Respond to yes/no questions related to living and nonliving objects and attributes

Vocabulary

alive	person	eat
pet	living	drink
roots	nonliving	breathe
animal	object	grow
plant		

Lesson 1—*(Introductory)* Living and Nonliving

This lesson should be done in a room that contains *no* living things except people.

Objective—To demonstrate an awareness that living things can do more than nonliving things

Procedure—

1. "I'm going to tell you something very important, so listen carefully. You are alive—you are a living thing. I am a living thing; *(child 1)* is a living thing; *(child 2)* is a living thing; *(child 3)* is a living thing; *(child 4)* is a living thing; *(child 5)* is a living thing." Ask each child, "Are you alive? Are you a living thing?"

2. "Now listen to this. The table is *not* alive. It is *not* a living thing." Ask each child, "Is the table alive? Is the table a living thing?"

3. Designate other nonliving things in the room. "The light is not alive; it is not living. The wall is not alive; it is not living. The chair is not alive; it is not living. This piece of paper is not alive; it is not a living thing." Ask the children to name other things in the room that are not alive. Conclude. "All of the people in this room are living. We are all alive. Everything else in this room (the chairs, the table, the pencils) is *not* alive—is *not* a living thing."

4. "Now think about all the things you can do. You are alive and can do so many things that this table cannot do." Have the children think of what they can do because they are alive. For each suggestion say, "Yes, you can _____ . You are alive. Can the table _____ ? No, the table cannot _____; it is not alive." Encourage the children to think of as many suggestions as possible.

5. Review. "Can living things do the same kinds of things as things that are not living? Can the table, which is not living, do the same kinds of things as we, who are living, can do?" Conclude. "Living things (people) can do many more things than things that are not living."

Lesson 2—*(Introductory)* Alive and Not Alive

Objective—To demonstrate an awareness of the characteristics of living things

Materials—

Crackers—one for each child
Cup of water—one for each child
Drinking glass
Pencil
Book

Procedure—

1. "Yesterday we talked about the many things we can do because we're alive." Review some of the children's ideas *(talk, walk, eat, breathe, see, hear).* "Today we'll talk about some of the things we need in order to stay alive."

2. "Remember when we studied air and discovered that we had air in our bodies? When we breathe, we take air in and then let it out again. If we stopped breathing, we wouldn't be alive any- more; we would die. If there weren't any air for us to breathe, we would die too. So we need air to stay alive." Have the children demonstrate breathing.

3. "We also need food to stay alive. The food we eat goes into our bodies, and our bodies use it to keep us strong and healthy." Hand each child a cracker to eat.

4. "Water is another thing we need to stay alive. If we didn't have water, we couldn't stay alive; we would die. We don't always drink just plain water. We eat a lot of foods that have water in them, and we drink a lot of things that have water in them. But if we didn't get water, we would die." Let each child drink a cup of water.

5. "What are the three things we need to stay alive? Yes, we need air, food, and water to stay alive. Air, food, and water also help us to grow. If something is alive, we said it needs food. How do we take food into our bodies? Yes, by eating. *All living things eat food.* We also said if something is alive, it needs water. How do we take water

into our bodies? Right, by drinking. *All living things drink water.* And we said living things need air. How do we take air into our bodies? Yes, by breathing. *All living things breathe air.*"

6. "If living things eat food, drink water, and breathe air, they grow. *All living things grow.*"

7. Review. "There are four things we've learned that living things do. They *(eat food)*, they *(drink water)*, they *(breathe air)*, and they *(grow)*."

8. Point to (one at a time) a glass, a child, a pencil, a book, a child, another child. As each is indicated, ask:

    a. "What is this?"

b. "Let's decide if it is alive."

c. "Does it drink water?"

d. "Does it eat?"

e. "Does it breathe?"

f. "Does it grow?"

g. Conclude. "It eats, it drinks water, it breathes, it grows." (Or, "It does not eat, it does not drink water, it does not breathe, it does not grow.")

h. "Is it alive or not alive?"

i. "Tell us one reason we know it is (or is not) alive?" *(It eats, drinks, breathes, grows—or doesn't do these.)*

Lesson 3—*(Reinforcement)* Sorting Pictures of Living and Nonliving Things

Objective—To sort pictures into two categories: things that are living and things that are not alive

Materials—

Pictures of Living Things—People (See preparation instructions below)

Pictures of Nonliving Things (See preparation instructions below)

Scissors

Construction paper

Paste

Preparing the materials—Reproduce the pictures of Living Things—People (page 98) and Nonliving Things (page 99). Mount the pictures on construction paper. Cut apart the pictures.

Procedure—

1. Review by asking each child, "Are you alive? Is the _____ (use a different nonliving object in the room for each child) alive?"

2. "Today we'll look at lots of pictures and decide if they are pictures of things that are living or not living." Show the pictures of living and nonliving things individually. "Here is a picture of something. What is it? Is the _____ living or *not* living?" If necessary, help the child to answer by reviewing the attributes necessary for a living entity—breathing, eating, drinking water, growing.

3. "Let's look at those pictures again. This time, we'll sort them into two piles. In one pile we'll put all the pictures of things that are living. In the other pile we'll put all the pictures of things that are *not* living." Show a picture, have the children decide if it is a picture of a thing that is living or not living, and have a child place the picture on the appropriate pile.

4. When the sorting is completed, review by pointing to each pile and asking, "Why did we put all these pictures together?"

Lesson 4—(Extension) Lots of Life

Objective—To demonstrate an awareness that animals and plants are living things

Materials—

A school pet, preferably a mammal

A plant

Two short stalks of celery (the upper portion containing leaves)

Two glasses of water
(See preparation instructions below)

Food coloring

Pictures of Living Things—Animals
(See preparation instructions below)

Pictures of Living Things—Plants
(See preparation instructions below)

Pictures of Living Things—People (from Lesson 3)

Pictures of Nonliving Things (from Lesson 3)

Scissors

Construction paper

Paste

Preparing the materials—

1. Add a few drops of food coloring to the water in one of the glasses.

2. Reproduce the pictures of Living Things— Animals (page 100) and Living Things—Plants (page 101). Cut apart the pictures. Mount each picture on construction paper.

Procedure—

1. "We know now that we are alive and that we need air, water, and food to stay alive. We also know a lot of things that are not alive. For instance, this table and this chair are not alive. But there are lots of living things in the world besides people. Today we'll learn about some other living things."

2. Bring out the pet. "What is this? Yes, it's a mouse. Do you suppose the mouse is alive? How can we decide?" Help the children recall that all living things eat, drink, breathe, and grow. If the mouse does those, it must be alive.

   a. "Does the mouse eat?" Feed the mouse a small morsel of food. Discuss how mice eat, using their mouths, like people.

   b. "Does the mouse drink?" Offer the mouse water. Discuss how mice drink by licking up water with their tongues. Like people, the mouse drinks water through its mouth.

   c. "Does the mouse breathe?" The children can see and feel the mouse's chest expand and contract as it breathes. Discuss how the mouse uses its nose in breathing.

   d. "Does the mouse grow?" Discuss how the mouse was a baby and grew larger as it ate, drank, and breathed.

   e. "Is the mouse alive?"

   f. "How do we know?" Review that it does four things that living things do.

3. "This mouse is an animal. All animals are alive. Do you know the names of any other animals?" Help the children to supply as many as they can. Show the animal pictures. Label each, and explain that each is an animal. Go back through the pictures and ask the children, "Is this a picture of a living thing?" If necessary, remind them, "All animals are living things. A _____ is an animal."

4. Show the plant. "What is this? Do you suppose this plant is alive? How can we decide?"

   a. "Does the plant breathe?" Discuss that although we cannot see the plant breathing, it does take air in and let air out.

   b. "Does the plant eat?" Explain that the plant has parts under the ground called *roots* that take food from the ground. The plant does not have a mouth like people and animals, but it does eat.

   c. "Does the plant drink?" Explain that the plant drinks the same way it eats; it takes water from the soil through its roots. Demonstrate how water travels up a plant from the root. Place a short stalk of celery with the leaves intact in a container of water to which food coloring has been added. The color will travel to the leaves as the stalk draws up water. Place a similar stalk of celery in a container of uncolored water so the children will be able to compare the original leaf color of the celery with the changed stalk. The next day, check both stalks to observe the movement of the water.

d. "Does the plant grow?" Have the children examine the plant and notice the small new leaves and the older larger leaves. Explain that the smaller leaves are new sprouts and eventually will grow to be as large as the other leaves.

e. "Is the plant a living thing?"

f. "How do we know?"

5. Show the plant pictures. "Look at these pictures. Each one shows a kind of plant. All plants are living things. We'll learn a lot more about plants later, but for now just remember that plants are living." Do not label the pictures; merely say, "This is a picture of a plant. Is this a picture of a living thing?"

6. Place four pictures on the table in front of each child in this order:

Child 1: animal, plant, nonliving object, person

Child 2: plant, person, animal, nonliving object

Child 3: person, nonliving object, plant, animal

Child 4: nonliving object, animal, person, plant

Child 5: animal, plant, nonliving object, person

"I gave each of you four pictures. Three of them are pictures of living things. One is a picture of something that is not living. Look carefully at the pictures. When you find the picture that shows something that is *not living,* give it to me."

Lesson 5—*(Extension)* Life Pictures

Objective—To locate pictures of living and nonliving things

Materials—Magazines containing pictures of plants, animals, and people—one for each child

Procedure—

1. Give each child a magazine. "There are lots of pictures in your magazine. I will tell you to find a special kind of picture. Look through your magazine, and when you find the picture, put your finger on it. Ready?"

2. Have all children complete the following series of directions. Help any child who has difficulty locating a specific picture. After each request has been filled, the children should close their magazines in preparation for the next request.

a. "Find a picture of something that is living." Help each child to identify the picture as a person, an animal, or a plant.

b. "Find a picture of something that is *not* a living thing."

c. "Find a picture of something that is *not* a living thing."

d. "Find a picture of something that is a living thing." Again, help each child to identify the picture as an animal, a person, or a plant.

Repeat this series until the children are able to follow the directions readily.

3. "We've been talking about three kinds of living things the last few days. We said plants are alive, animals are alive, and people are alive. I'm going to give you some new directions to follow. These will be harder, so you'll have to think and look carefully. Ready?"

a. "Find a picture of something that is alive and is an animal."

b. "Find a picture of something that is alive and is a plant."

c. "Find a picture of something that is living and is a person."

d. "Find a picture of something that is living but is *not* a person."

e. "Find a picture of something that is alive but is *not* an animal."

f. "Find a picture of something that is living and is an animal."

g. "Find a picture of something that is living but is *not* a plant."

h. "Find a picture of something that is *not* alive."

Repeat any directions with which children had difficulty.

Living Things—People

Nonliving Things

Living Things—Animals

Living Things—Plants

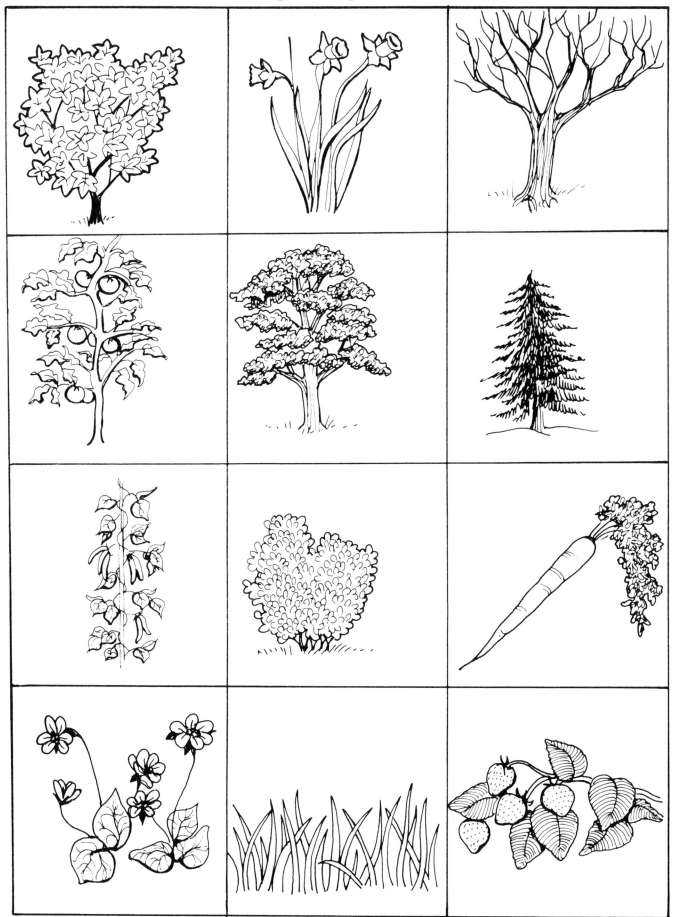

Unit VII
Plants and Plant Growth

This unit is best carried out at a time of year when plants are in growth.

Language Development—
Goals, Objectives, and Vocabulary

Goals

To increase naming vocabulary of common plants in the surrounding environment

To improve classification and sequencing skills

Objectives

Receptive

The student will:

1. Identify plants presented by name (tree, bush, or flower)

2. Recognize different attributes of plants, such as color, size, and fragrance

3. Classify parts of a plant including flower, stem, leaves, roots, and trunk

4. Comprehend the sequence of plant growth from seed to full-grown

Expressive

The student will:

1. Label plants presented as tree, bush, or flower

2. Label common plants in the surrounding environment

3. Label parts of a plant including flower, stem, leaves, roots, and trunk

4. Respond to a question in a complete sentence, using a negative when appropriate

Vocabulary

tree	leaves
shrub	root
bush	trunk
fragrance	above
bloom	below
flower	bean
stem	seed
leaf	

Lesson 1—*(Introductory)* Plants

Objective—To identify a plant

Materials—Plant pictures (See preparation instructions below)

Preparing the materials—Reproduce the plant pictures (pages 110-113). Color each picture and mount it on construction paper.

Procedure—

1. "We've looked at a few pictures of plants before, but today we're going to look at pictures of many, many plants and learn about some of the different kinds of plants."

2. Show the 20 plant pictures individually. "Each of these plants has a name. I will tell you some of the names." Label each plant as a tree, a shrub (bush), or a flower. For plants common to the area, give the common name also. "This is a picture of a tree. A tree is a plant. This kind of tree is an *oak* tree." Do not name uncommon plants.

3. "Let's go outside now and look for plants. When you see a plant—any kind of plant—tell us so we can all look at it." Help the children to notice plants outdoors and to label them as trees, shrubs (bushes), small plants, or flowers. Encourage them to feel the plants (the roughness of bark, the textures of leaves). Have them smell fragrant plants and note size and color differences.

Lesson 2—*(Introductory)* Plant Parts

Objective—To identify flowers, stems, and leaves

Materials—

Flowering plant in a pot
Flower pictures (from Lesson 1)
Tree pictures (from Lesson 1)
Red, blue, and green crayons—
   one set for each child
Tree Worksheets—one for each child
Flower Worksheets—one for each child

Preparing the materials—Reproduce the Tree Worksheet (page 114) and the Flower Worksheet (page 115). Make a set for each child.

Procedure—

1. "Yesterday we looked at different kinds of plants. Today we're going to find out some ways in which plants are alike."

2. Show the flowering plant in a pot. "We'll look at this plant first. This plant has *flowers* on it; it is in bloom right now." Have each child point to the flower part of the plant. "Let's see what other parts it has."

   a. "This part is called the *stem.*" Have each child point to the stem. As the child does so, ask, "What is that part?"

   b. "This part is called a *leaf.* The plant has many leaves." Have each child point to a leaf. As the child does so, ask, "What is that part?"

3. Take the children outside to look at a tree.

   a. "This plant is a tree. Are there any flowers on this tree?" If there are no flowers, explain that the tree is not in bloom but sometimes it does have flowers.

   b. "This part is the stem." Have each child point to the stem. As the child does so, ask, "What is that part?" Inform the children that the stem of the tree is called the *trunk.* Discuss how much larger the tree stem is than the flower stem is.

   c. "This part is a leaf." Have each child point to a leaf. As the child does so, ask, "What is that part?"

4. Return to the classroom. "We've learned three parts of plants so far. We've seen *(flowers)*, and *(stems)*, and *(leaves)*. Do all plants have flowers? Yes, all plants have flowers, and all plants also have leaves."

5. Show each flower picture. Have the children take turns pointing to the flower, the stem, and the leaves on each picture.

6. Show each tree picture. Have the children take turns pointing to the stem and the leaves on each picture.

7. Give each child a Tree Worksheet and a red and blue crayon.

   a. "Find your red crayon and mark the stem on that plant."

   b. "Find your blue crayon and mark a leaf on that plant."

8. Give each child a Flower Worksheet and a green crayon (in addition to the red and blue crayons).

   a. "Find your red crayon and mark the stem on that plant."

   b. "Find your blue crayon and mark a leaf on that plant."

   c. "Find your green crayon and mark a flower on that plant."

Lesson 3—*(Introductory)* Roots

Objective—To show an awareness of plant roots

Materials—

Two flowering plants in pots
Access to weeds and grass growing outdoors

Procedure—

1. "What plant parts have we learned so far? *(stem or trunk, leaves, flowers)* Today we'll learn about a part that we can't see because it is under the ground."

2. Show the two flowering plants in pots. Have the children label the stem, leaves, and flowers.

3. Cut one flower, stem, and leaves from one of the potted plants. "This flower has been cut from this plant, and it no longer has an important plant part. Watch what happens." Attempt to place the cut flower upright on the table. The plant will fall over. "What happened? Yes, it fell over. Does this plant *(potted plant)* fall over? No, it doesn't fall over because part of it is in the soil, and that holds it up and keeps it from falling over."

4. Take the class outside. Show the children the grass. "Grass is another kind of plant. Does the grass fall over or stand up? Yes, the blades of grass stand up, so there must be something holding the plant up. Let's see what it is." Carefully pull out several blades and show the children the roots. Explain that this part of the plant is called the *root*. Have the children repeat the word. Point to the soil attached to the roots.

Pull up a weed to show how long some roots are. Compare the height of the weeds and the length of the roots, and compare the height of the grass and the length of its roots. Help the children conclude that the size of the roots varies with the size of the plant.

5. Return to the classroom. "Do you suppose if we pulled this potted plant out of the ground the way we pulled out the grass, we would see roots? Do you think this plant has roots? Yes! And one thing the roots do is help to keep the plant from falling over."

6. Show the cut flower. "Does a cut flower have roots? No, when this stem was cut off of the plant the roots stayed in the ground."

7. "There is something else the roots do besides hold up the plant. The roots also take food and water from the soil and feed the plant." Have the children recall the soil they saw attached to the roots on the weeds and grass. "We know that plants need food and water to stay alive." Indicate the cut flower and the potted plant. "One of these will not be able to stay alive because it will not be able to get food and water. Which of these will die? Yes, the cut flower will die. Why? Yes, it will die because we cut it off from its roots and it won't be able to get food and water. We'll check tomorrow to see what has happened." Place the plants aside. Have the children check them the next day and observe that the cut flower has wilted. Discuss again the functions of the plant roots and the reasons for the wilting and dying of the cut flower.

8. Conclude. "We learned two things about roots. They *(help hold the plant upright)* and they *(supply food and water to the plant from the soil)*."

9. "Now you will have a chance to pretend to be plants." Ask one child to pretend to be the stem and stand up straight. Ask a second child to pretend to be the roots and move into a position in relation to the "stem." Let the children decide by themselves where the "roots" should be and

how the child can look most like a root. Repeat this procedure for the leaves and flowers. When all the plant parts are in place, ask, "Who is the stem? Are you above the ground or below the ground? . . . Who is the root? Are you above the ground or below the ground? . . . Who are the leaves? Are you above the ground or below the ground? . . . Who are the flowers? Are you above the ground or below the ground?"

Lesson 4—(Reinforcement) Growing Plants

Objective—To show how a bean plant grows by sequencing four pictures

Materials—

Plastic transparent drinking glasses marked with the child's name—one for each child plus five for demonstration plants

Bag of potting soil

Spoon or scoop

Pitcher of water

Presoaked lima beans
(See preparation instructions below)

Bean Sequence Picture Sets
(See preparation instructions below)

Bean Sequence Chart
(See preparation instructions below)

Construction paper

Paste

Scissors

Seeds—five different kinds (grass seeds, orange seeds, apple seeds, radish seeds, morning glory seeds)

Preparing the materials—

1. Place dried lima beans (3 for each child, 15 for the demonstration plants) in a container. Cover with water to a level 3″ above the beans. Soak the beans overnight.

2. Reproduce the Bean Sequence Picture Set (page 116). Make one copy for each child and one copy for the Bean Sequence Chart.

3. Mount each Bean Sequence Picture Set on construction paper. Cut the pictures apart into four cards each.

4. To make a Bean Sequence Chart, cut apart one Bean Sequence Picture Set and mount the four pictures on a piece of construction paper 18″ x 24″. Place the pictures in order from left to right across the page.

Procedure—

1. "We know four plant parts. We've talked about the stem, the leaves, the flowers, and the roots. Today we're going to learn a new part—seeds."

2. Show the five different kinds of seeds, naming each. "These are all seeds from plants. They are parts of the plants. If we planted these seeds and took care of them, they would grow into new plants. The apple seeds would grow into apple trees, the grass seeds would grow into grass, . . ." Conclude. "The plant that grows will vary, depending on the seeds that are planted. Would an orange tree grow if we planted radish seeds? No, an orange tree would grow only if we planted orange seeds."

3. "Today we're going to plant beans. If we take care of them, they'll grow into plants. What kind of plant will they grow into? Yes, a bean plant."

4. Examine a soaked bean that has opened in the center. Show the children the tiny plant and leaves contained inside the bean. Have them notice how the outer coating of the seed is split by comparing the soaked bean with a dried bean. "When we plant a seed in the soil and

water it and give it sunlight, it will grow. The tiny plant inside the seed will come out and grow above the soil, and we'll be able to see it. Tiny roots will grow down into the soil, but we usually can't see them."

5. Help each child plant bean seeds.

   a. Place 2″ of potting soil in the plastic glass.
   b. Place three soaked beans on top of the soil.
   c. Cover the seeds with soil to ½″ from the top of the glass.

6. While the children watch, plant three seeds in each of the additional five glasses. Explain to the children that these will be used for experiments about plants.

7. "Now our seeds are planted, but they won't grow unless we take care of them. Remember when we talked about what living things need to stay alive? Let's think now and try to remember what our plants will need to stay alive." Discuss the following:

   a. Water. Allow the children to water their seeds. Be careful not to overwater, or mold will develop.
   b. Food. Discuss the fact that the food for the plant is already in the soil. When roots grow, they will take in food for the plant.
   c. Air. Have the children recall that air is all around the room. After the plants grow, they will have no trouble getting air.
   d. Sunlight. Plants need sunlight. Place the seeds in their cups in sunlight so that when the plant begins to grow it will have sunlight.

8. Show the Bean Sequence Chart.

   Picture 1: "First we plant the bean seeds, just as we did today. Tiny bean plants are inside these seeds right now, even though we can't see them."

   Picture 2: "In a few days the seeds will begin to open up like this. Part of the tiny plant will grow down into the soil."

   Picture 3: "Soon the roots will form, and the whole bean will come out of the ground as the stem grows and pushes up. The leaves will begin to come out."

Picture 4: "Finally, our plants will look like this." Review the roots, the stem, and the leaves. Point out the remnant of the seed. Place the chart on the wall or bulletin board where the children will be able to see it.

9. "I'll give each of you four pictures. Put the picture that shows the bean seeds on top of the others. As our plants grow, we'll change the pictures. In a week or so, when our plants have grown, I'll ask you to put your pictures in order to show how a bean plant grows." Help each child select Picture 1 and place it on top of the other pictures. Each child should then place the picture stack next to the plant.

Each day, when the children water their plants, help them decide if the top picture should be changed. If the stage illustrated in Picture 2 is not visible in any glass after three days, uproot one of the demonstration plants to show the children how their beans look now. Have them place Picture 2 on top of the other pictures beside the plant.

10. One or two days after the plants have reached the stage shown in Picture 4, review the sequence of bean growth individually with each child. Refer to each child's Bean Sequence Picture Set. "Here are the four pictures that show how your plant changed as it grew. Let's put them in order to show how it grew."

   a. "How did the bean look when you first planted it? Hand me the picture that shows how it looked when you planted it."
   b. "Now hand me the picture that shows what happened next."
   c. "Hand me the picture that shows what happened next."
   d. "Hand me the picture that shows how your plant looks now."
   e. As the child hands you the pictures, place them on the table in sequence from left to right.
   f. Briefly review the sequence with the child.

Lesson 5—(Reinforcement)
Plant Life

Objective—To demonstrate an awareness of the four things plants need to stay alive

Materials—

Four of the demonstration bean plants (from Lesson 4)

Each child's plant (from Lesson 4)

Pitcher of water

Procedure—

1. "Today we're going to talk a little more about what plants need to stay alive." Ask the children to tell four things plants need. Have the children study their own plants as the discussion continues.

   a. "Is your plant getting water? How?" *(The children are watering them; the roots are bringing the water to the rest of the plant.)*

   b. "Is your plant getting air? How?" *(Air is all around.)*

   c. "Is your plant getting food? How?" *(There is food in the soil; the roots are bringing the food to the rest of the plant.)*

   d. "Is your plant getting sunlight? How?" *(The plants are placed by the window.)*

2. Present the four additional plantings. "Yesterday these beans also had air and water and sunlight and food, but today I'm going to put these plants in special places. We'll do an experiment to see what happens."

3. Take one plant to a closet or very dark area. "I'm going to put this plant in the closet. I'll water it first. Each day I'll give it some water, but I'll leave it in the closet. Will it have air? *(Yes.)* Will it have water? *(Yes.)* Will it have food? *(Yes.)* Will it have sunlight? *(No.)* What do you think will happen to this plant if it doesn't have sunlight?" Explain that they will watch for a week to see what happens to a plant without sunlight.

4. Take a second plant to the closet. "I'm going to put this plant in the closet also. But I'm not going to water it. Will it have air? *(Yes.)* Will it have food? *(Yes.)* Will it have sunlight? *(No.)* Will it have water? *(No.)* What do you think will happen to this plant if it doesn't have water or sunlight?"

5. Place the third plant in the sunlight. "I'm going to put this plant here in the sunlight, but I'm not going to water it. Will it have air? *(Yes.)* Will it have food? *(Yes.)* Will it have sunlight? *(Yes.)* Will it have water? *(No.)* What do you think will happen to this plant if it doesn't have water?"

6. Place the fourth plant in the sunlight. "I'm going to put this plant here in the sunlight, and I'm going to water it each day." (Water the plant) "Will it have air? *(Yes.)* Will it have food? *(Yes.)* Will it have sunlight? *(Yes.)* Will it have water? *(Yes.)* What do you think will happen to this plant?"

7. "We're going to watch what happens to these four plants. Each day we'll look at each of these plants to see what is happening." Review the growing conditions for each of the four plants. Visit each plant as you talk about these. "Remember, this plant will have food and air and sunlight and water . . . This plant will have food and air and sunlight, but no water . . . This plant will have food and air and water, but no sunlight . . . This plant will have food and air, but no sunlight and no water." Ask the children to predict what will happen to each of the plants. Record their predictions.

8. Check each plant each day. Be sure to water only the two plants where water was specified. Discuss the changes with the children. Compare these changes with their predictions. Allow them to change any prediction.

Lesson 6—*(Extension)* Plant Pictures

Objective—To locate plants in a picture of an outdoor scene

Materials—Magazine pictures of outdoor scenes (see preparation instructions below)

Preparing the materials—Collect five or six full-page magazine pictures of outdoor scenes showing a variety of plants (trees, shrubs, flowers) in an urban setting. Mount each picture on construction paper.

Procedure—Show and discuss each outdoor scene. "These pictures show many different plants. Let's look at this picture and see how many different plants we can find." Have the children point to the various plants. Label each as a tree, a shrub, or a flower. Discuss other details of the picture that are *not* plants. For example, if there is a house in the picture, ask, "Is this a plant?" Use a complete sentence to state the answer: "No, this is *not* a plant; it is a *house*." It is important for the children to hear negative forms in sentence patterns.

Lesson 7—*(Extension)* Flower Parts

Objective—To dissect flowers and label their parts

Materials—

Three or more different types of flowers with leaves—one sample of each type for each child and adult

One each of two different types of flowers.

Procedure—

1. Present one flower. Ask the children to tell you what kind of flower it is (or, if necessary, label it). Then help them label the stem, leaves, petals, and "center section" of the flower. This center section is the reproductive part of the flower, consisting of stamens and pistils. It is not necessary for young children to be able to label these parts. You might have them rub the pollen off the tips of the stamens.

2. Hand each child a flower. Help the children to locate the stem, leaves, petals, and center section. They might take their flowers apart to find all the sections.

3. Repeat the procedure with two or more other types of flowers.

Plants

Plants

Plants

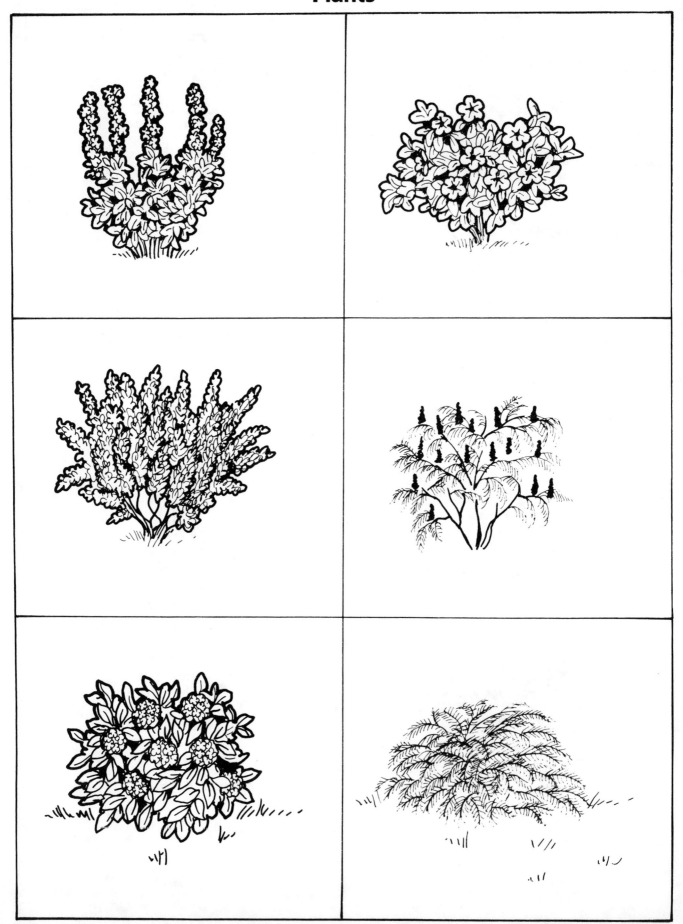

Plants

Tree Worksheet

Flower Worksheet

Bean Sequence Picture Set

Unit VIII
Fruits and Vegetables

Ten fruits and ten vegetables are included in this unit. Others may be substituted or added. Lessons on fruits and lessons on vegetables are interspersed, following the curriculum format of Introductory, Reinforcement, and Extension Lessons. You may prefer to teach all fruit lessons first, all vegetable lessons second, and then the lessons dealing with both fruits and vegetables.

Language Development— Goals, Objectives, and Vocabulary

Goals

To establish a basic vocabulary foundation and to increase the ability to recall specific vocabulary

To improve categorization skills while increasing the ability to associate fruits and vegetables with their properties and characteristics

Objectives

Receptive

The student will:

1. Match fruits and vegetables to the appropriate pictures

2. Associate the meaning of *plant* with *fruit* and *vegetable*

3. Classify fruits and vegetables in a sorting activity

4. Comprehend differences between the concepts *raw* and *cooked* as they relate to eating and preparing vegetables

Expressive

The student will:

1. Label parts of various fruits and vegetables

2. Respond to yes/no questions regarding properties of fruits and vegetables

3. Describe fruits and vegetables according to shape, color, and texture

4. Compare similarities and differences of fruit group and vegetable group

5. Label fruits and vegetables in a tactile activity involving the sense of touch only

6. Name products made from various fruits and vegetables

7. Label fruits and vegetables upon presentation of object and picture

8. Compare similarities and differences between pairs of fruits and vegetables

9. Respond to yes/no questions related to characteristics or attributes of fruits and vegetables

Vocabulary

fruit	peel	pear	raw	husk	potato
vegetable	seeds	cherry	cooked	rain	radish
plant	membrane	strawberry	corn	field	celery
apple	sweet	peach	carrot	fresh	cauliflower
banana	sour	pineapple	peas	frozen	broccoli
orange	core	lemon	stalk	canned	lettuce
juice	stem	bunch of grapes			

Lesson 1—*(Introductory)* Fruits

Objective—To match fruits and their pictures

Materials—

Two red apples
Two bananas
Two oranges
Pictures of fruits
  (See preparation instructions below)
Knife
Paper napkins

Preparing the materials—Reproduce the pictures of fruits (pages 127-129). Color the pictures and cut them apart.

Procedure—

1. "We've been talking about plants, how they grow, what they need to grow, and the many different kinds of plants there are. One kind we haven't talked about is the plants that we can eat. For the next few weeks we'll be learning about plants that we eat."

2. Show an apple, banana, and orange. "Here are three kinds of things we can eat. They all grow on trees. They are all part of the plant. They are all *fruit*. Does anyone know the name of this fruit? Yes, this fruit is an orange. Does anyone know the name of this fruit? Yes, this fruit is an apple. Does anyone know the name of this fruit? Yes, this fruit is a banana."

3. Show each fruit again and ask, "What is the name of this fruit?"

4. Show the orange and discuss its color, shape, and texture. Cut the orange so each child has one wedge. Discuss the parts of the orange that are now visible *(peel, seeds, juice, membrane)*. "Do we eat the peel? Do we eat the seeds?" Have the children taste the orange. "How does it taste?" *(sweet, sour)* As they taste it, ask: "What is the name of the fruit you are eating?"

5. Show the apple, discuss it, and have the children taste it. Point out the peel, seeds, core, stem. Point out that we usually eat the peeling of an apple. As the children taste it, ask, "What is the name of the fruit you are eating?"

6. Show the banana, discuss it, and have the children taste it. As they taste it, ask, "What is the name of the fruit you are eating?"

7. Show the fruit pictures. "Here are pictures of the fruits we just tasted." Show the second set of fruits. "Let's match the real fruits with the pictures of the fruits."

    a. "This is an *(orange)*, so we'll put it on top of the picture of the orange."
    b. "This is a *(banana)*, so we'll put it on top of the picture of the banana."
    c. "This is an *(apple)*, so we'll put it on top of the picture of the apple."

8. Allow each child to match the fruits with their pictures. Place the pictures in a row in front of the child. Hand the fruits, one by one, asking the child to place each on the appropriate picture.

Conduct similar introductory lessons for the other fruits and for the vegetables that are taught in this unit. As additional fruits and vegetables are presented, use a cumulative review. For example, when lemons and grapes and cherries have been added to the fruit group, review those in combination with apple, orange, and banana.

Lesson 2—*(Introductory)* Vegetables

Objective—To participate in preparing vegetables for eating

Materials—

Pictures of vegetables
   (See preparation instructions below)
Pictures of growing vegetables
   (See preparation instructions below)
Scissors
Two cobs of corn with husks
Carrots with leaves attached
Peas in pods
Hot plate
Pan containing water
Knife
Paper napkins
Plastic spoons

Preparing the materials—Reproduce the pictures of vegetables (pages 130-132) and growing vegetables (pages 133-134). Color the pictures and cut them apart.

Procedure—

1. "We've learned the names of many fruits. Today we're going to begin talking about another kind of plant we eat—vegetables. There are many fruits and many vegetables."

2. Show the corn, a carrot, and the peas. Identify each and explain that each is a vegetable.

3. Show the picture of corn growing in a field. "Corn is a kind of plant. Here is a picture of corn growing in a field." Discuss what can be seen in the picture—the stalks, the leaves, the cobs in the husks. "If corn is a plant, what does it need to grow?" Review the information from the plant growth unit. Discuss how the plant gets each of these essentials. Emphasize that water for plants growing outside is supplied by rain.

4. Show and discuss the pictures of the carrots and the peas growing in the same way.

5. Show the three fresh vegetables again. "These vegetables are *raw* right now. We usually don't eat them raw. We usually cook them first. Just like the fruits, some of the vegetables have to be peeled and prepared before we eat them."

a. Shell the peas. Explain that the pod is not usually eaten. Give each child a raw pea to taste. "Is that pea raw or cooked? How does it taste? Do you usually eat peas raw?"

b. Husk the corn. Explain that the husk, the cob, and the silk are not eaten. With the knife, remove a kernel of corn for each child to taste. "Is that corn raw or cooked? How does it taste? Do you usually eat corn raw?"

c. Remove the leaves from the carrot, wash it, and give each child a slice to taste. "Is that carrot raw or cooked? How does it taste? Do you usually eat carrots raw? Yes, the carrot is a vegetable that we eat raw and cooked."

6. "We've tasted these three vegetables raw. Now we'll cook them and see how they taste." Dice the carrot. Remove the corn from the cob. Place the raw vegetables in water in the pan and place it on the hot plate. "What will happen to the water in the pan? What happens to water when it is heated? Yes, it will get hot and it will boil. As the water boils, the vegetable will cook. Let's watch and see." As the children observe the formation of steam, review the liquid and gas forms of water. Review the names of the vegetables being cooked. Ask, "Are peas fruits or vegetables? Are bananas fruits or vegetables? Are carrots fruits or vegetables? Are apples fruits or vegetables? Is corn a fruit or a vegetable? What color are peas? What color are carrots? What color is corn?"

7. When the vegetables are cooked, give the children a taste of each. Discuss what happened when the vegetables were cooked. *(They became soft.)* As the child tastes each vegetable, ask, "What is the name of that vegetable? Is the _____ raw or cooked?"

Conduct similar introductory lessons with the other vegetables. The children should learn that some vegetables (such as lettuce and radishes) are always eaten raw, some may be eaten raw or cooked, others are always eaten cooked. Experiences with frozen and canned vegetables will help the children to become aware that we do not always buy our vegetables fresh (or raw).

Take a trip to a farm or garden where the children can see vegetables growing. A trip to an orchard is helpful when studying fruits. Radishes grow relatively quickly and can be planted from seeds in a container in the classroom. Individual plants can be uprooted from time to time to show the growth and development of the radish.

Throughout the introductory lessons in this unit, emphasize that fruits and vegetables are *plants* which

are grown and eaten. Although only two introductory lessons are described in this unit, a week or more (five or more lesson plans) should be spent introducing the vegetables (or fruits) before proceeding to reinforcement and extension lessons. Despite the repetitious format, the children's interest is maintained by the new foods introduced each day.

Lesson 3—*(Reinforcement)* Dot-to-Dot Fruit

Objective—To complete and identify dot-to-dot pictures of fruits

Materials—

Pictures of fruits—banana, strawberry, pineapple, orange, pear, apple (from Lesson 1)

Dot-to-Dot Fruit Pictures
(See preparation instructions below)

Crayons for each child

Preparing the materials—Reproduce the Dot-to-Dot Fruit Pictures (pages 135-140). Make one set for each child.

Procedure—

1. Show the fruit pictures one by one and ask, "What is the name of this fruit?"

2. Show the dot-to-dot banana picture. "Here is a picture of one of the fruits we just saw. This pic-

ture isn't finished. We have to use a crayon and go from dot to dot to finish the picture. What do you think it will be if we finish it?" Demonstrate how to follow the dots with a crayon to complete the outline. Give each child a crayon and a dot-to-dot banana picture. Help the children to complete their pictures. When each child's picture is complete, ask, "What fruit is that?"

3. Follow the same procedure to complete the strawberry, pineapple, orange, apple, and pear dot-to-dot pictures.

4. Allow the children to color the completed dot-to-dot pictures. The pictures can be used to help the children decide what color each of the fruits should be.

Children will enjoy similar lessons with dot-to-dot vegetable pictures.

Lesson 4—*(Reinforcement)* Fruit Touch

Objective—To identify a fruit by touch

Materials—

One of each fruit—apple, orange, peach, pear, pineapple, banana, lemon, bunch of grapes
Blindfold
Box

Procedure—

1. "Today we're going to play a guessing game. We're going to try to guess which fruit is in this box by touching it. We'll use only our sense of touch. Who would like to have the first turn?"

2. Blindfold one child. Place a fruit in the box. Have the child place one hand in the box, bring out the fruit, and handle and feel it. "What is the name of that fruit?" If the child cannot

answer correctly after several attempts, remove the blindfold and let the child see the fruit. Have the children take turns until the eight fruits have been identified by touch.

3. Place the eight fruits on the table. Review their names. "This is a . . . ? This is a . . . ? Now I'm going to give each of you a turn to name all the

fruits by touching them. You'll have to think hard!" Blindfold one child. Present each fruit and ask the child to name it. Give each child a turn. Vary the order in which the fruits are presented to each child.

A similar identification game can be played with vegetables.

Lesson 5—*(Reinforcement)* Fruit Names

Objective—To name fruits

Materials—

Large mixing bowl
Paper plate and paper dish or cup—
    one for each child
Large serving spoon
Plastic spoon and plastic knife—
    one set for each child
Paper napkins
One orange
One apple
One banana
Jar of maraschino cherries
Can of pears
Can opener

Procedure—

1. Have the children wash their hands. "Today we are going to prepare fruit salad. What are some things we could put in our fruit salad?" Help the children to recall as many fruit names as they can. "Should we put a potato in our fruit salad? Why not?"

2. Show the fruits and have the children identify each. The pears can be identified by the picture on the can.

3. "Each of you will cut up one fruit to put in our fruit salad." Let each child select a fruit by name. Give the child the fruit, a plastic knife, and a paper plate.

4. Discuss how to prepare each fruit (the orange will need to be peeled, the apple must be cored, . . .). Have the children prepare and cut the fruits and place them in the large bowl. Give assistance as needed.

5. Mix the cut-up fruit in the bowl. Give each child a dish or cup of fruit salad and a plastic spoon. Have the children identify the various fruits as they eat the salad. "Let's all put a piece of banana on our spoons." When each child has located a banana, say "What is the name of that fruit? Now let's eat the banana. What fruit do you have on your spoon, Joe? Yes, a piece of pear. Can everyone find a piece of pear?"

In similar lessons children can prepare a tossed salad and vegetable soup.

Lesson 6—*(Reinforcement)* Fruit Juice

Objective—To match fruits and juices

Materials—

Fruits—three oranges, one of each—grapefruit, lemon, tangerine, apple
Fruit juices in pitchers—apple juice, grapefruit juice, lemon juice, tangerine juice

Bowl
Knife
Paper cups
Paper plates—one for each child
Crayon

Procedure—

1. "Today we're going to talk about juices that are made from fruits." Show the oranges. "First we'll

make some juice from this fruit. What is the name of this fruit?" Slice the three oranges in half. Give each child a half. Ask the child to squeeze the juice into the bowl. Give each child a taste of the juice. "Where did we get the juice we just tasted? Yes, the juice was in the orange and we squeezed it out. What kind of juice was it? From which fruit did we get it? Right! We got orange juice from oranges."

2. "Many fruits are used to make fruit juices. We'll taste some fruits and some juices made from them. We've talked about two of these fruits, but two of them are fruits we haven't talked about before."

3. Place the four fruits on the table. "Let's name the fruits first. This is an *(apple)*, this is a *(lemon)*, this is a *(grapefruit)*, and this is a *(tangerine)*."

Supply the name for any fruit the children cannot name, and have them repeat the word.

4. Discuss the fruits in terms of color, size, and so on. Point out that these fruits all have peels.

5. Cut each fruit into wedges and give each child a portion on a paper plate. Have the children smell each fruit as they receive it. Ask the

children to "Point to the apple . . . Point to the grapefruit . . . Point to the lemon . . . Point to the apple . . . Point to the tangerine . . . Point to the apple . . . Point to the lemon . . . Point to the grapefruit."

6. Label four cups A, B, C, and D for each child. Pour a small amount of apple juice in the A cups, grapefruit juice in the B cups, lemon juice in the C cups, and tangerine juice in the D cups. Give each child the four juice samples. "Each of the juices I gave you was made from one of these fruits. Let's find out which juice was made from which fruit."

7. Instruct each child to take a small sip of juice from Cup A. Then have the children take a small taste of each fruit and decide from which fruit the juice was made. Have each child place Cup A beside the appropriate fruit. Continue until the children have matched the remaining juices and fruits. Review by pointing to each pair and saying, "Apple juice is made from apples, grapefruit juice is made from grapefruit, . . ."

8. Let the children drink the juices and eat the fruits.

Lesson 7—(Reinforcement) Potatoes

Objective—To participate in various preparations of potatoes

Materials—

Potatoes—two raw, one warm baked, potato chips, package of frozen french fries
Cooking oil
Frying pan
Pan containing water
Hot plate with two burners
Milk
Fork or potato masher
Knife
Potato peeler
Mixing bowl
Paper plates and spoons—one for each child
Paper napkins

Procedure—

1. Show a raw, unpeeled potato. "What is the name of this vegetable? Do we eat potatoes like this or do we do something to them first? Yes, we cook the potato. We can cook it in different ways and make different kinds of potatoes."

2. "First, let's taste the raw potato." Peel the potato and give each child a small piece to taste. Have the children notice that it is hard and crunchy.

3. Dice the remaining potato and peel and dice the second raw potato. Place the potatoes in the pan containing water. "We'll cook the rest of the potato by putting it in water and boiling it." Place the pan on the hot plate. While the potatoes cook, discuss the other potato forms.

4. Show the baked potato. "This is a potato I cooked before you came to school. I didn't peel it and I didn't cut it up and put it in water. I

washed it and put it in the oven in the stove. The heat from the oven cooked it. It's called a baked potato, because I baked it in the oven." Let each child taste a piece of the baked potato including the peeling. Discuss how baking made the potato soft. Compare its texture to the hard and crunchy raw potato.

5. Show the frozen french fries. "Here is another way potatoes can be fixed. These are called french fries. To make french fries, we peel the potato and cut it into pieces like this. Then we put the pieces in some oil in a pan and fry them." Fry the potatoes. Have the children taste the cooked french fries. Discuss how frying made the potato soft.

6. By this time the boiled potatoes should be soft enough to eat. Give each child a taste. Have the children recall that these potatoes were *boiled* in water. Discuss the softness of the potatoes.

7. Explain that boiled potatoes are used to make mashed potatoes. "We can eat boiled potatoes the way we just did, or we can make mashed potatoes out of them. To make mashed potatoes, we mash the boiled potatoes with a fork or

masher." Place the remaining boiled potatoes in the mixing bowl and mash them. "Then we add a little milk and mash some more." Give each child a small amount of mashed potato to taste. Discuss the softness and the change in the appearance of the potatoes.

8. Show the potato chips. "Here is another way we eat potatoes. We usually buy the potatoes this way at the store, but they are made from raw potatoes. The potatoes are peeled and sliced very, very thin. Then they are salted and cooked in oil until they're crispy. What is the name of this kind of potato?" Have each child taste a potato chip. Comment particularly on the salty taste.

9. Review. "We've eaten potatoes prepared in different ways today. What kinds of potatoes did we eat?" Help the children recall the raw potato, the potatoes that were baked, boiled, and mashed, and the french fries and potato chips.

Similar lessons may use other vegetables or fruits and their products (for example: apples, apple sauce, apple juice, apple pie, apple butter).

Lesson 8—*(Reinforcement)* Fruits and Vegetables

Objective—To distinguish between fruits and vegetables

Materials—

Pictures of fruits (from Lesson 1)
Pictures of vegetables (from Lesson 2)
Two tables
Small basket or paper sack

Procedure—

1. "Today we're going to play a game called Store. First we have to set up the store. We will sell fruits and vegetables in our store. I have many pictures of fruits and vegetables, but they're all mixed up. We need to sort them. We'll put all the fruit pictures on this table and all the

vegetable pictures on this table." Hold up each picture. Have the children identify it and decide if it is a picture of a fruit or a vegetable. Place the picture on the appropriate table. Continue until all the pictures are sorted.

2. "Now our store is ready. Who would like to be the first shopper?" Hand the child the basket and give shopping instructions. "Go to the store and buy an apple and a banana." Have the child visit the store, choose the correct pictures, place them in the basket, and return to the group. With the group, check to see if the child bought the items requested. "What was Tim supposed to buy at the store? Yes, an apple and a banana. Did he? Let's check." Ask another child to return the pictures to the appropriate tables. Continue to play the game until each child has had two turns to shop for two items. Vary the shopping

instructions to include two fruits, two vegetables, or a fruit and a vegetable. Have the pictures replaced on the appropriate table after each turn.

3. When the children are familiar with the game, specify only the category of the foods to buy.

  a. "Go to the store and buy one fruit and one vegetable."

  b. "Go to the store and buy one vegetable and two fruits."

  c. "Go to the store and buy one vegetable and one fruit."

  d. "Go to the store and buy two fruits and one vegetable."

  e. "Go to the store and buy three vegetables and one fruit."

Lesson 9—*(Extension)* Shopping

Before this lesson, make arrangements with a grocer. Explain the purpose of the shopping trip and obtain cooperation.

Objective—To identify fruits and vegetables

Procedure—

1. On the day before this lesson, explain to the children that they will be going to the store to buy fruits and vegetables. Make a shopping list of fruits and another list of vegetables by asking the children to name fruits and vegetables they might buy and writing their responses. Read back the two lists.

2. Take the children to a grocery store. Visit various areas and point out how the store is arranged (all the cereals are together, all the canned foods are together, . . .).

3. Visit the fresh fruit and vegetable section. Show the children all the fruits and vegetables they have studied. While showing each, ask, "What is this? Is it a fruit or a vegetable?" Also show the children examples of fruits and vegetables that were not studied. "This is another vegetable. It is a _____."

4. Visit the canned goods area. Point out that we can usually tell what is in the can by looking at the picture on the outside. Using cans with pictures, show the children all the available examples of the fruits and vegetables they have studied. For each, show the can and ask, "What is in this can? Is it a fruit or a vegetable?"

If money is available, allow each child to buy one fruit or one vegetable (either fresh or canned) to bring back to school where it can be prepared and eaten by the children or sent home with the child. Some of these foods could be used for Lesson 10.

Lesson 10—*(Extension)*
Like Fruits and Vegetables

Objective—To state how fruits and vegetables are alike

Materials—

Fresh fruits—banana, orange, apple, lemon
Fresh vegetables—potato, carrot, radish, lettuce
Box
Gummed stars

Procedure—

1. Place the orange, apple, lemon, and banana on the table. "We already know one way these are all alike (the same). We've learned that all of these are *(fruits)*." Place the potato, carrot, radish, and lettuce on the table. "And we know one way in which these are all alike. They are all *(vegetables)*. Today we'll be thinking about other ways in which these foods are alike."

2. Return all the fruits and vegetables to the box. Place the orange and lemon on the table. "Think hard and tell me how these two are alike." When someone names a way that the two fruits are alike, let that child put a gummed star on each fruit. If the children cannot think of any answers or seem confused by the question, explain that the orange and lemon are alike because they are both fruit. "The orange is a fruit, and the lemon

is a fruit." Ask, "Can we eat the lemon? Can we eat the orange? Then what is another way they are alike? Yes, both of them can be eaten." Let someone put a star on each fruit. Have the children try to think of a third way these fruits are alike. Ask questions, if necessary, to help them reach conclusions about similarities. *(Both are fruits, both can be eaten, both have seeds, both have peels, both can be bought at the store, both grow on trees, both can be made into juice, . . .)* If the children suggest *differences* ("One is orange and one is yellow"), explain, "That is a way they are *different*. They are not both yellow, so that can't be a way in which they are alike. Try to think of a way in which they are *alike*." After each suggestion, let that child put another gummed star on each fruit. When four or five similarities have been identified, review them. Return the lemon and orange to the box.

3. Present and discuss similarities of other pairs. Allow the children to put on gummed stars after they make suggestions.

   a. Banana and apple *(Both are fruits, both can be eaten, both have peels, both are bought in a store, both grow on trees.)*

   b. Lettuce and radish *(Both are vegetables, both can be eaten, both are usually eaten raw, both can be bought in a store.)*

   c. Potato and carrot *(Both are vegetables, both can be eaten, both can be eaten cooked, both can be bought in a store, both foods grow underground.)*

   d. If children have difficulty, present additional pairs.

4. Method of presentation:

   a. Show the pair, and ask, "How are these alike? How are they the same?"

   b. Check the child's response by saying: "Is the _____ (first food) _____ (characteristic)? Is the _____ (second food) _____ (characteristic)? Yes, they are both _____ (characteristic), so that is one way in which they are alike." Or, "No, they are not *both* _____ (characteristic), so that is not a way in which they are the same."

   c. Verify all similarities named by the procedure outlined above.

   d. After several similarities have been established, review. "We said these are alike because they both _____ and _____ and _____ and _____."

   e. Remove the pair and present a new pair.

Extend the lesson by establishing similarities among three or more foods.

Lesson 11—(Extension) Fruit and Vegetable Cards

Objective—To play a card game to conclusion in a cooperative manner

Materials—
Fruit and Vegetable Card Game
  (See preparation instructions below)
Construction paper
Paste
Laminating materials
Scissors

Preparing the materials—Reproduce the pictures of fruits and vegetables (pages 141-142). Make four copies of each. Mount the pictures on construction paper. Laminate them, and cut them apart to make 40 playing cards.

Procedure—

1. "Today we're going to play a card game. I'll shuffle the cards and deal them out. When you get your cards, look to see which fruits and vegetables you have." Shuffle the cards. Deal four to each child and place the remaining cards in a stack, face down on the table.

2. "Each of you has four cards." Have each child place the four cards face up on the table. Ask each child in turn to name the items pictured on the cards. "We'll try to make sets of pictures that are alike. There are four pictures of each fruit and four pictures of each vegetable. Try to get four of one kind to make a set. We'll keep playing until all the cards are in sets."

3. "This is how to play. Tim, you start. Look at your cards. Choose one of them and ask Laura *(the child to the left)* to give you *all* her bananas *(or other fruit or vegetable Tim has chosen)*. Laura, look at your cards and give Tim all the banana cards you have. Tim, put the cards with the other banana cards. When you have four of them, turn them over face-down on the table. Laura, if you don't have any banana cards, tell Tim 'Go to the garden.' Tim, if Laura tells you to go to the garden, take a card from the face-down stack in the center of the table and put it with your other cards. Then it's Laura's turn to choose a fruit or

vegetable and ask for cards from the person sitting next to her."

4. Begin playing the game. Explain the rules again as the need arises.

5. Continue playing the game until the pile in the center of the table is gone and no one can take a turn, or when all sets have been formed.

6. Collect and shuffle the cards. Play the game a second time. This time, have the children hold their cards so the others can't see them (rather than placing them face up on the table). Give help as needed.

Lesson 12—(Extension) Vegetable Prints

Objective—To choose the vegetable called for in verbal directions

Materials—

Sets of vegetables
  (See preparation instructions below)
Paper plates and paper bowls—one of each
  for each child
Red paint
Smocks—one for each child
Large sheets of construction paper

Preparing the materials—

1. On a paper plate, assemble the following vegetables. Make a set of vegetables for each child.
   3″ piece of celery stalk
   ½ of a small head of cabbage
   ½ of a potato
   1 radish
   1 cauliflower floweret

2. Cut a simple design (O, X, T,) into the flat side of the potato.

3. Cut the radish so it will have a flat side. Then cut a design into the flat side.

4. Fill the paper bowls with ½″ of red paint.

Procedure—

1. Show each of the vegetables and have the children label them. Ask, "Were the things I just showed you fruits or vegetables? Are they raw or cooked?"

2. Give each child a set of the vegetables. "Today we're not going to eat the vegetables; we are going to print with them." Point out the designs cut into the potato and radish. "First, let's make sure everyone remembers the names of the vegetables. Please hold up the piece of cauliflower. Hold up the radish. Hold up the piece of cabbage. Hold up the piece of celery. Hold up the piece of potato."

3. Demonstrate how to print with the vegetables. "Watch, and I'll show you how to use the vegetables to print." Choose a vegetable. Dip the flat side down in the paint. Press the vegetable, paint side down, onto the paper. Several prints can be made without redipping the vegetable into the paint.

4. Give each child a piece of paper and a dish of paint. Begin as a group by having the children print with each vegetable according to directions (that is, all children will make a radish print, a cauliflower print, a cabbage print, ...). Give help as needed.

5. Provide clean sheets of paper and allow the children freedom to make their own designs with the vegetables. As they work, discuss the vegetables they are using.

Fruits

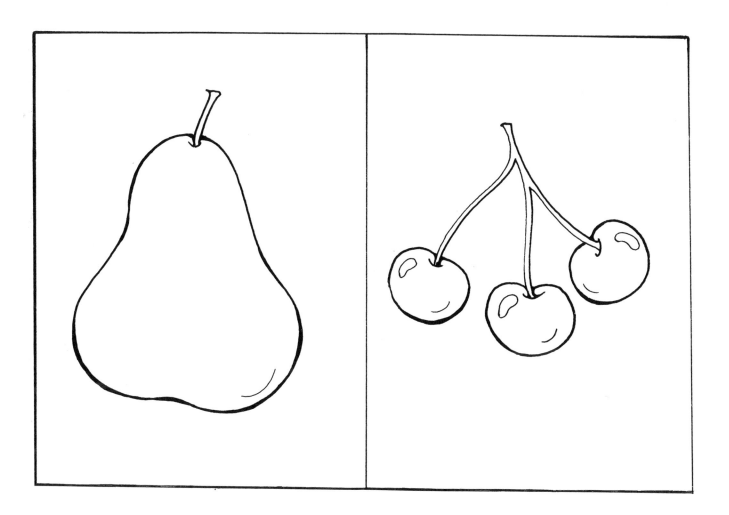

Fruits

Fruits

Vegetables

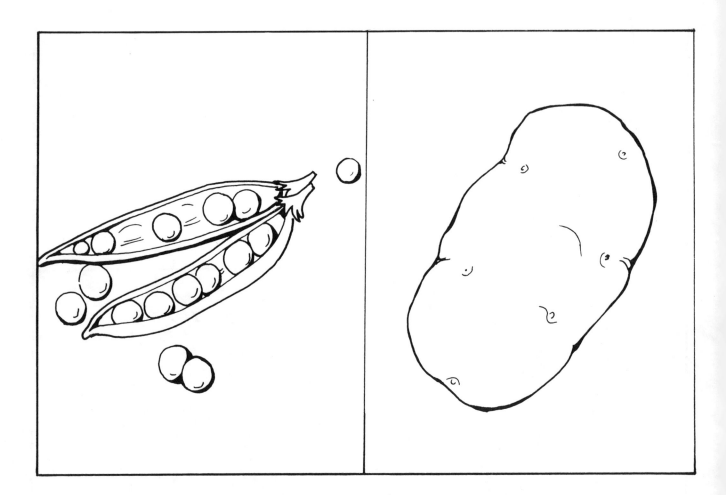

Vegetables

131

Vegetables

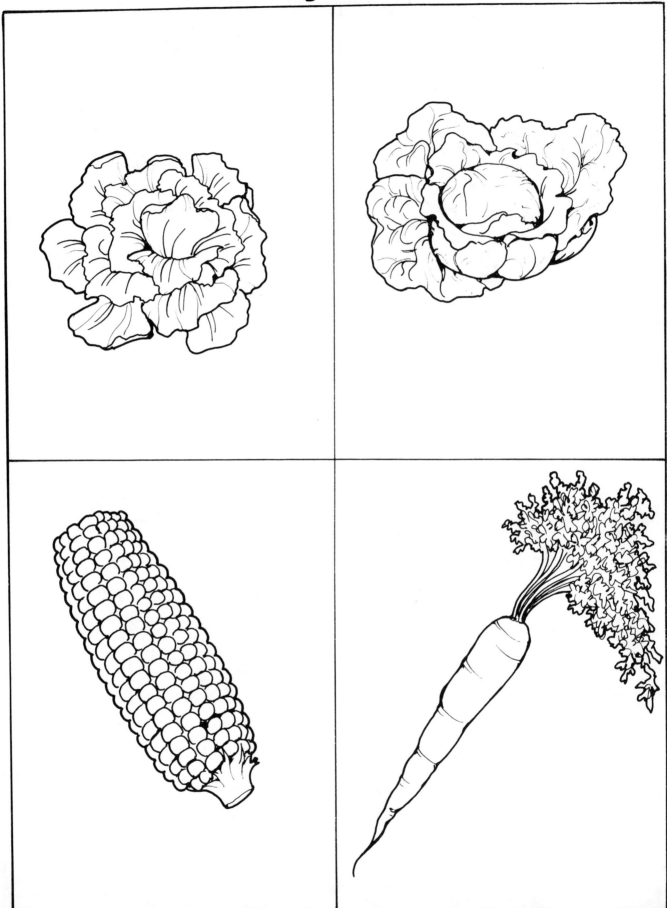

Growing Vegetables

Growing Vegetables

Dot-to-Dot Fruit

Dot-to-Dot Fruit

Dot-to-Dot Fruit

Dot-to-Dot Fruit

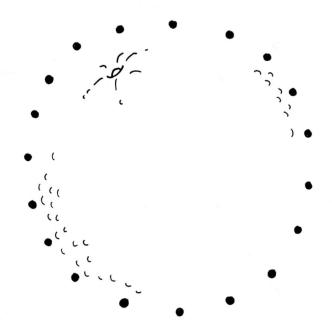

Dot-to-Dot Fruit

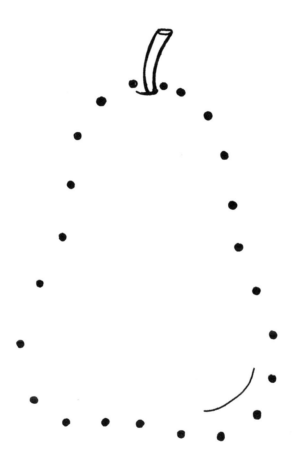

Dot-to-Dot Fruit

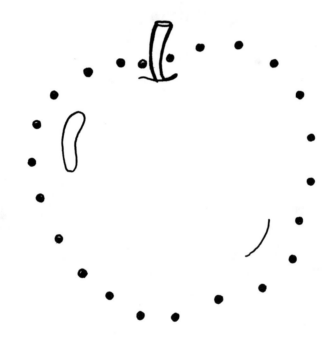

Fruit and Vegetable Cards

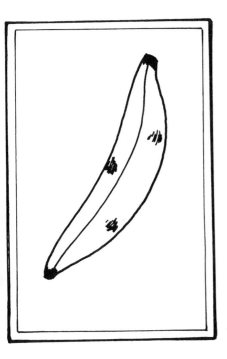

Fruit and Vegetable Cards

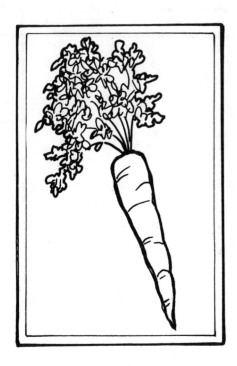

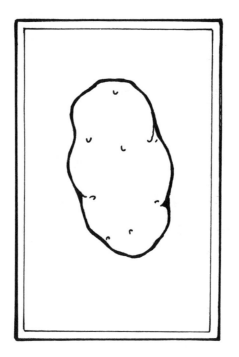

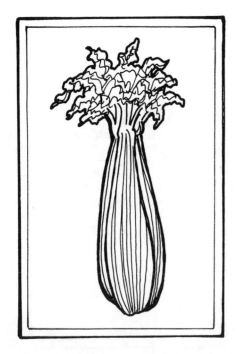

Unit IX
Nutrition, Health, and Safety

Because this unit deals with three distinct areas (nutrition, health, safety), the lesson plans are arranged according to the areas rather than according to the type of lesson (Introductory, Reinforcement, Extension). Use the plans as starting points to develop other plans that expand each of these areas according to the children's needs and experiences.

Language Development— Goals, Objectives, and Vocabulary

Goals

To comprehend the concepts of nutrition, health, and safety and their relationship to everyday situations

To increase ability to classify situations as healthy/nonhealthy and safe/unsafe in order to improve decision-making skills

Objectives

Receptive

The student will:

1. Classify foods as dairy, cereal, meat, fruit, or vegetable

2. Comprehend the concepts of *healthy* and *unhealthy*

3. Classify foods as healthy or unhealthy

4. Sort foods into three categories (breakfast, lunch, dinner)

5. Comprehend the meaning of the concepts *clean* and *dirty*

6. Comprehend the meaning of the concepts *safe* and *unsafe* (or *dangerous*)

7. Comprehend and recognize the difference in the meaning of stoplight colors red, yellow, and green

8. Physically express actions that should be taken by cars and by people at a traffic light as colors change

Expressive

The student will:

1. Express a conclusion based on facts related to healthy and unhealthy habits in a story activity

2. Classify situations as safe and unsafe

3. Express rules that should be considered when crossing a street

4. Verbally express actions that should be taken by cars and by people at a traffic light as colors change

Vocabulary

cereal	dairy products	dinner	gutter
wheat bread	fruit	vitamin	corner
white bread	vegetable	protein	stop
cottage cheese	healthy	calcium	slow
American cheese	unhealthy	tooth	go
milk	sick	teeth	traffic
air	meal	toothbrush	traffic light
food	breakfast	street	stoplight
water	lunch	crosswalk	

Lesson 1—(Introductory) Eating Well

Objective—To state which of two children in a story is more likely to get sick and which child ate the proper kinds of food for a meal

Materials—

Box of dry cereal
Slice of whole wheat bread
Slice of white bread
Quart of milk
Cottage cheese
American cheese
Cooked bacon
Two hard-boiled eggs
Cooked hamburger patty
Apple
Carrot
Paper napkins
Paper cups
Chalkboard and chalk

Procedure—

1. "Are you alive? What do you need to stay alive?" *(Food, water, air)*

   "We've been studying about two kinds of foods. What were they? *(fruits and vegetables)* Yes, fruits and vegetables are foods. There are many other kinds of foods, too. Some foods are very good for our bodies because they help keep us healthy and feeling good so we can play and think and work and have fun. If we don't eat the right kinds of foods we may be too tired or too sick to do those things. Let's try to name as many foods as we can. Think hard about all the different foods you eat. When you have an idea, I'll write it on the chalkboard so we'll be able to remember all the ideas." Have the children name as many foods as they can. Write each idea on the board. When the list is complete, read it back to the children.

2. "Very good! You thought of lots of foods! I brought some foods to school today. They are the kinds of food our bodies need to stay healthy."

   a. Show the milk, cottage cheese, and American cheese. "These foods help us have strong bones and teeth. They are foods made from milk, and they are called dairy products." Have the children identify (or identify for them) the foods and taste a small portion of each of the three foods. "We should eat some of this kind of food each day."

   b. Show the dry cereal and bread. Have the children identify and taste a small portion of each. "We should eat some of this kind of food each day. These are called cereal products."

   c. Show the cooked bacon, hard-boiled eggs, and cooked hamburger patty. Have the children identify and taste a small portion of each. "We should eat some of this kind of food each day. These foods are meat and egg products."

   d. Show the carrot and apple. Have the children identify and taste a small portion of each. "We should eat some of this kind of food each day. These foods are . . . ? Yes, these are fruits and vegetables."

3. Return to the food list on the chalkboard. Allowing the children to contribute as much as they are able, identify each food on the list as primarily a dairy product, a cereal product, meat and eggs, or fruits and vegetables. Ask the children to supply additional examples of foods in each category.

"Each kind of food does something for us. Some foods help our bones and teeth, some foods help our hair and fingernails, some foods help our eyes, and some foods help our skin. There are lots of foods and lots of parts to our bodies. To keep all the different parts of our bodies healthy, we need to eat lots of different kinds of foods."

"Suppose we ate only candy. Do you suppose our bodies would stay healthy? What might happen?" *(Get cavities in teeth, get fat, get weak bones)*

"Suppose we ate only bread. Do you suppose our bodies would stay healthy? What might happen?" *(Get fat, get tired, get sick)*

"Would our bodies stay healthy if we ate only hamburger?"

Conclude. "In order to keep our bodies healthy, we need to eat all kinds of foods. We need milk and meat and fruits and vegetables and breads and many other foods."

4. "I will tell each of you a story about two children. One didn't eat the right kinds of food, and the other did eat the right kinds of food. Listen carefully because I'm going to ask you which child might get sick." Read one story to each child.

Story 1. "John ate bacon and eggs and orange juice and milk for breakfast. Sam ate a candy bar for breakfast. Listen again." Repeat the story. "Which child might get sick because he didn't eat the right kinds of food? *(Sam)* Which child ate the right kinds of food for breakfast?" *(John)*

Story 2: "Susan ate a lollipop for lunch. Karen ate a hamburger and peas and potatoes and milk for lunch. Listen again." Repeat the story. "Which child might get sick because she didn't eat the right kinds of food? *(Susan)* Which child ate the right kinds of food for lunch?" *(Karen)*

Story 3: "Carol ate cereal and milk and an apple for breakfast. Judy chewed a piece of bubble gum for breakfast. Listen again." Repeat the story. "Which child might get sick because she didn't eat the right kinds of food? *(Judy)* Which child ate the right kinds of food for breakfast?" *(Carol)*

Story 4: "Joe drank a soda for supper. Jimmy ate vegetable soup and milk and a salad for supper. Listen again." Repeat the story. "Which child might get sick because he didn't eat the right kinds of food?" *(Joe)* Which child ate the right kinds of food for supper?" *(Jimmy)*

Story 5: "Tammy ate a piece of cake for lunch. Ann ate a cheese sandwich, a glass of milk, and an apple for lunch. Listen again." Repeat the story. "Which child might get sick because she didn't eat the right kinds of food? *(Tammy)* Which child ate the right kinds of food for lunch?" *(Ann)*

Lesson 2—*(Reinforcement)* Meals

Objective—To identify pictures of three meals as breakfast, lunch, and dinner

Materials—

Paper breakfast, lunch, and dinner foods (See preparation instructions below)
Marking Pens
Scissors
Paper plates—one for each child and one for the teacher

Preparing the materials—Reproduce the pictures of breakfast, lunch, and dinner foods (pages 151-153). Make a copy for each child. Color the pictures and cut them apart.

Procedure—

1. Give each child a paper plate. "Today we are going to eat some pretend meals. The first meal we'll pretend to eat is breakfast. Each of you has

a plate. I'll serve the food. What is the name of the meal we are going to eat? Yes, breakfast. When do we eat breakfast? Right, breakfast is the meal we eat when we get up in the morning." Give each child an egg; ask, "What is that?" Give each child a piece of toast; ask, "What is that?" Give each child an orange; ask, "What is that?" Give each child a glass of milk; ask, "What is that?"

Have the children pretend to eat the foods. Discuss how each is eaten—with a fork, a spoon, or your hands. Collect the pictures as the foods are "eaten."

Review. "What meal did we eat? When do we usually eat breakfast? What foods did we eat for breakfast?"

2. "Another meal we eat is lunch. We eat lunch in the middle of the day." Discuss lunchtime in terms of the children's school day. "I have a pretend lunch for you. Would you like to eat it? Get your plates ready!" Pass out the paper lunch foods and follow the procedure used with breakfast: Have the children identify each food as it is passed out; discuss how these foods are eaten and have the children pretend to eat them; collect the pictures; review ("What meal did we eat? When do we usually eat lunch? What foods did we eat for lunch?").

3. "Another meal we eat is dinner (supper). We eat dinner near the end of the day." Discuss dinner

in terms of the children's school and home schedules. "I have a pretend dinner for you. Would you like to eat it? Get your plates ready!" Pass out the paper dinner foods and proceed as before.

4. Review. "We've pretended to eat three meals. What were they? We pretended to eat all kinds of foods, so we should be nice and healthy now! Eating three meals a day will help us stay strong and well."

5. If time permits, discuss and help the children as a group sort one set of the paper foods eaten for the three meals into four groups: dairy products, cereal products, meat and eggs, fruits and vegetables.

The material in Lessons 1 and 2 should be reinforced throughout the school year by using the words *breakfast, lunch,* and *dinner (supper)* with the children during informal discussions. Ask the children from time to time what they ate for breakfast that morning or for dinner the day before. If lunch is served in school, discuss at that time the variety of foods served, the body's need for a variety of foods, and the names of the foods. Discuss *why* it is important to eat certain foods. Expose the children to words such as *vitamins, protein,* and *calcium* to convey the idea that there are "things" in food that are good for our bodies.

Lesson 3—(Introductory) Brushing Teeth

Objective—To brush teeth properly

Demonstration teeth and the large toothbrush usually are available from a dentist. When you arrange to borrow them, ask the dentist to show you how to brush the teeth properly. Opinions vary.

Sample kits of toothbrushes and toothpaste may be available free from dentists or drugstores. For children who eat meals in school, try to obtain two kits—one to keep at school and one to send home.

Materials—

Large demonstration set of teeth and toothbrush
Toothbrushes—one for each child
Tubes of toothpaste—one for each child
Paper cups

Procedure—

1. "Remember when we learned that milk helps us to grow big and strong? We also said that milk helped us to have strong bones and teeth. Well, there are some other things we need to do to help us have good, strong teeth. We need to eat the proper foods and brush our teeth often."

2. Using the demonstration set of teeth and the large toothbrush, show the proper way to brush

teeth. Explain as you demonstrate. "The teeth on top are brushed down, like this . . . The teeth on the bottom are brushed up, like this . . . Brush between the teeth, inside and out . . . Clean the chewing parts of your teeth by scrubbing like this." Using the demonstration set of teeth and toothbrush, have each child practice the proper brushing procedure.

3. Explain to the children that if teeth are not brushed, they can get holes in them. "The holes are called cavities. If the cavities get big, our teeth will hurt when we try to eat, and we will need to go to the dentist to have the cavities filled. There are many ways we can get holes or cavities in our teeth, but the one thing that makes cavities the quickest is to leave food in our mouths—not brushing our teeth after we eat. We should brush our teeth after we eat to get the food out from between our teeth so our teeth will not get cavities. We should brush our teeth after breakfast, after lunch, and after dinner. We should brush our teeth after we eat a snack. It's a good idea to brush our teeth before we go to bed at night, too."

4. Give each child a toothbrush. Write the child's name on the toothbrush. Have the children practice proper brushing with water only. Offer help. Then give each child a tube of toothpaste. Let the children brush again, using toothpaste.

5. For at least two weeks, continue to have the children brush their teeth at school each day. If a snack is served, have the children brush after eating. Provide close supervision and remind them of the proper brushing procedure. Frequently ask the children why it is important for them to brush their teeth.

Lesson 4—(Introductory) Washing Before Meals

Objective—To wash before school meals regularly

Materials—

Washable doll
Large bowl of water with soap, washcloth, and towel
Paper towels
Small bars of soap—one for each child

Procedure—

1. Put the doll in the bowl of water. Use the soap, washcloth, and towel to wash and dry the doll as you ask the children, "Do you ever wash your bodies? Why do you suppose people wash themselves? Why do you suppose we should wash?" Help the children think of reasons. *(Because we get dirty, so we won't smell, so we'll look nice, to get clean)*

2. Let the children take turns washing the doll. As they work, discuss the reasons for washing. "One important reason why we wash ourselves is that there are germs all around. Germs are very, very tiny—so tiny we can't even see them." Remind the children that we can't see air but know it is all around us. "Germs get on our bodies and in our bodies. They can make us sick. They can make our bodies have an unpleasant smell. So we wash our bodies, and when we do we wash off the germs. The germs keep coming back, so we have to wash again and again."

"An especially important time to wash our hands and faces is before we eat. When we play and work, we get dirty lots of times. So before we eat, we should wash our hands and faces so the dirt and germs from them will not get on our food and inside our bodies. Besides, it looks nicer to come to the table with clean hands and faces. We like to look at each other when we look nice."

3. Take the children to the sink. Give each child two paper towels—one for washing and one for drying. Hand out the bars of soap. Show the children how to lather the paper towel and how to wash, rinse, and dry their faces. Remind them to close their eyes so soap will not get in them. Have the children practice washing their faces.

4. Show the children how to wash their hands by lathering them with soap and rubbing, rinsing, and drying them. Have the children practice washing their hands.

5. For at least one week, have the children wash their hands and faces before eating, using the paper towels. Each time, discuss the procedures and their importance. If the children eat meals at school, have them continue to wash their hands and faces before eating each day. Teach them how to wash their faces without a washcloth by first washing and rinsing their hands, then relathering and washing their faces with their hands.

Lesson 5—*(Introductory)* Safety

Objective—To identify a picture that shows a safe way for walking outside and a picture that shows an unsafe way for walking outside

Materials—Safety Pictures (See preparation instructions below)

Preparing the materials—Reproduce the Safety Pictures (pages 154-159).

Procedure—

1. "We've talked about how we need to eat certain foods in order to stay alive and healthy. We've also talked about how we need to take care of our bodies by brushing our teeth and washing ourselves to stay healthy. But there are some other things we need to do to take care of ourselves so we won't get sick or hurt ourselves. For instance, we must be careful not to touch hot stoves and burn ourselves. We don't jump out of windows because we might break our bones. There are lots of things we must do so we can stay safe. Today we'll talk about ways to stay safe when we are outside on the street."

   "When you are playing or walking outside, what must you remember to do so you won't get hurt?" The children should be able to supply some ideas from what their parents have told them. *(Don't play in the street, watch out for cars, don't go out of the yard, . . .)* Discuss the children's ideas.

   "When you go for a walk, there are things to remember so you won't get hurt or hurt others. You want to get where you are going safely."

2. Ask a child to stand up and walk to you with eyes closed. Just before the child bumps into something, ask the child to stop. Ask the other children what would have happened if the child had kept walking. *(The child would have bumped into something.)* Ask them why the child would have bumped into something. *(The child's eyes were closed.)* Conclude. "So one of the things you must remember when you are walking is to keep your eyes open."

   Select another child and ask, "What is one thing you must do when you are walking?" *(Keep your eyes open.)* Tell the child to walk backwards with eyes open; that is, to walk away from the others but keep looking at them. Just before the child bumps into something, ask the child to stop. Ask the children, "Tell me something else you must do when you are walking on the sidewalk." *(Look to see where you are going.)*

3. "Besides keeping your eyes open and looking to see where you are going, there are some other rules we must know for safe walking." Hold up Picture 1 (walking on a sidewalk) and say, "One rule is to walk on the sidewalk, *not* in the street." Give the picture to a child and say, "Tell the others what the picture reminds us to do." *(Walk on the sidewalk and not in the street.)* Have the other children repeat the answer in unison.

   Repeat Step 3, using Pictures 2 and 3 (crossing at a corner and using a crosswalk).

   Show Picture 4 (crossing in the middle of a block). "This picture shows something we should *not* do when we go walking. We should *not* cross the street in the middle of the block, because we might not see a car that is coming and the driver might not see us."

Discuss Pictures 5 and 6 (walking in a gutter and not using the crosswalk) in the same way.

4. Take the children on a walk in an area where there are corners, crosswalks, and sidewalks.

Discuss good safety habits. Then cross the street, emphasizing these habits. In the middle of the block, ask the children, "If I want to cross the street, what should I do?" *(Go to the corner.)* Then proceed to the corner and cross with the children.

Lesson 6—*(Reinforcement)* Street Safety

Objective—To state two things one should remember when walking outside or crossing a street

Procedure—

1. "We know some things we should remember when we are walking outside. We know we should walk on the sidewalk; we know we should cross the street at the corner; we know we should cross between the lines of the crosswalk. Today we'll talk about some other things to remember."

   "Suppose I'm walking on the sidewalk and I come to the corner and just keep walking across the street." Walk, without stopping, to demonstrate. "What might happen to me? Yes, I could get hit by a car. Before we cross the street, we need to *stop.*"

   "Suppose I'm walking on the sidewalk and I come to the corner and stop, and then I cross the street." As you talk, demonstrate by walking, then stopping, but keeping your eyes straight ahead. "Would that be a safe way to cross the street? Why not? What should I do after I stop?" *(Look in both directions to make sure no cars are coming.)*

2. "I know a little poem to help us remember what to do. Listen and I'll teach it to you." Begin walking and say, "Stop *(stop),* look *(look to the right and then to the left),* and listen *(put your hand behind your ear as if listening)* before you cross the street. Use your eyes *(point to your eyes)* and use your ears *(point to your ears)* before you use your feet *(point to your feet and resume walking).*" Have the children repeat the words and motions after you several times:

Stop, look, and listen
Before you cross the street.
Use your eyes and use your ears
Before you use your feet.

3. Take the children on a walk. Cross a street at a corner with a stop sign and a crosswalk. At the corner, repeat the poem to help them remember to stop, look, and listen. After pointing out that no cars are coming, cross the street. Cross back in the same manner.

   Point to the stop sign. "Here is something that helps keep us safe. It is called a stop sign." Point out that the word says STOP. "It tells the cars to stop before they cross the street." Observe the cars stopping for the sign. Point out that the drivers look before crossing the street just as people who are walking must do. Observe other pedestrians crossing the street and point out those who follow correct and incorrect crossing procedures.

   Visit a corner that has a stoplight and a crosswalk. Explain that the stoplight also helps cars and people cross in safety. Observe the traffic and the pedestrians as the colors change. Return to the classroom.

4. Work individually with each child at a distance from the group. "Tell me two things you should remember to do when walking outside or crossing the street." There are many possible answers. *(Keep your eyes open, stop at a corner, don't walk in the gutter, walk on the sidewalk, look both ways before crossing the street.)* Accept any reasonable answers. If the child supplies only one answer, say, "Yes, that's one thing. What is another thing you should remember?"

Lesson 7—(Extension)
Stoplight Safety

Objective—To respond correctly to traffic lights

Materials—

Stoplight Pattern
(See preparation instructions below)
Construction paper—black, red, yellow, green
Scissors
Paste

Preparing the materials—

1. Reproduce the stoplight patterns (pages 160-161). Use black construction paper for the base; and red, yellow, and green construction paper for the circles. Cut out the pieces. Make one set for each child and one extra for demonstration.

2. Assemble the demonstration stoplight:
   a. Cut out the colored circles and paste them in place on the stoplight base.
   b. Cut out the circle on the strip.
   c. Cut slits along the dotted lines on the stoplight base, above and below the lights.
   d. Insert the strip through the slits to cover the lights as needed.

Procedure—

1. "Yesterday we looked at stoplights and stop signs, and we learned that they help keep people safe on the street by letting them know when to stop and when to go. Today we'll make paper stoplights. Then we'll play a game with them."

   Show the demonstration stoplight. "This stoplight, like the one we saw outside, has three colors on it." Show each color by moving the strip. "It has a _(red)_ light, a _(yellow)_ light, and a _(green)_ light. Each color tells us and the cars to do something."

   Show the red light. "The red light is at the top. It means we should stop. What does the red light tell us to do?" Show the yellow light. "The yellow light is in the middle. It means be careful—slow down and get ready to stop. What does the yellow light tell us to do?" Show the green light. "The green light is at the bottom. It means we can go. What does the green light tell us to do?" Quickly review the three colors and their meanings.

2. Give each child the materials to make a stoplight. Help the children to assemble their stoplights.

3. When the stoplights are completed, play the traffic game. Have the children stand in a line about seven feet from you. "I am going to change the traffic light. You pretend to be a car and do what the light tells you to do." Show the red light. "What should you do right now? Yes, the light is red, so no one should be moving—all the cars are stopped." Show the green light. "Now what should the cars do? Why?" Show the yellow light. "What should the cars do? Why?" Show the red light. "What should the cars do? Why?"

4. Have the children return to their original positions seven feet from you. Play the game again. The children may choose to be different things this time—people walking, trucks, bicycles.

5. Play the game a third time. "This time I'm not going to ask you what to do or tell you what color the light is. Just watch the light and do what it says." Play the game by changing the light, but do not discuss each change. Observe the children's ability to do what is indicated by the light.

6. If time permits (or during directed play), the children may take turns being the teacher and changing the traffic light. They also may use toy trucks or cars to respond to the light.

7. Have the children follow these directions, using their own stoplights: "Make your stoplight say GO. Make your stoplight say STOP. Make your stoplight say SLOW DOWN." Repeat the three directions several times in varied order.

Breakfast

Lunch

Dinner

Safety Picture 1

Safety Picture 2

Safety Picture 3

Safety Picture 4

Safety Picture 6

Stoplight Pattern

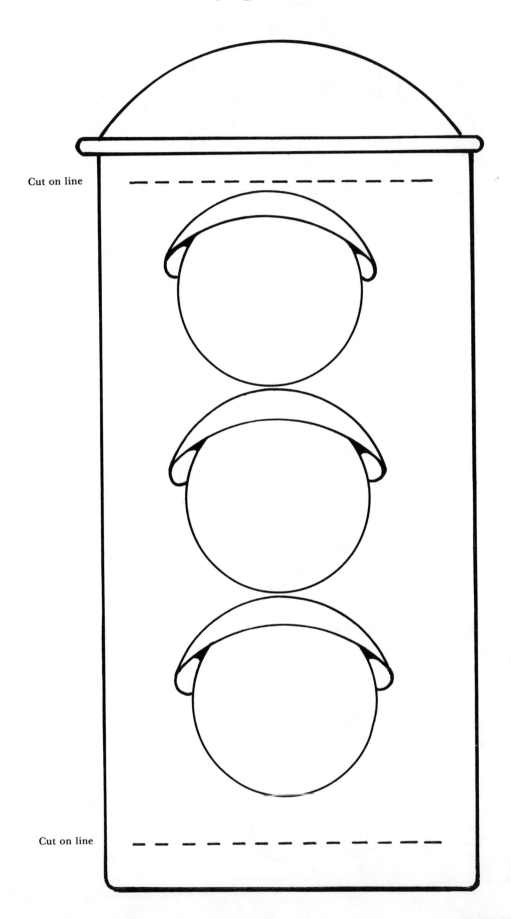

Cut on line

Cut on line

Strip Insert and Circle Patterns for Stoplight

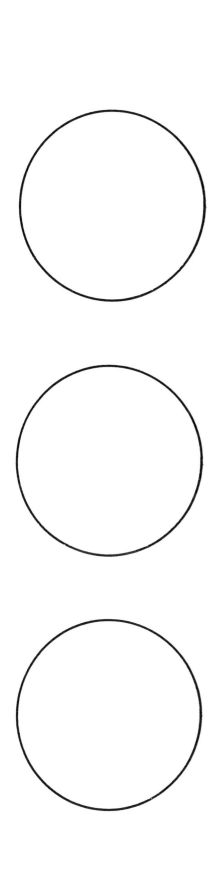

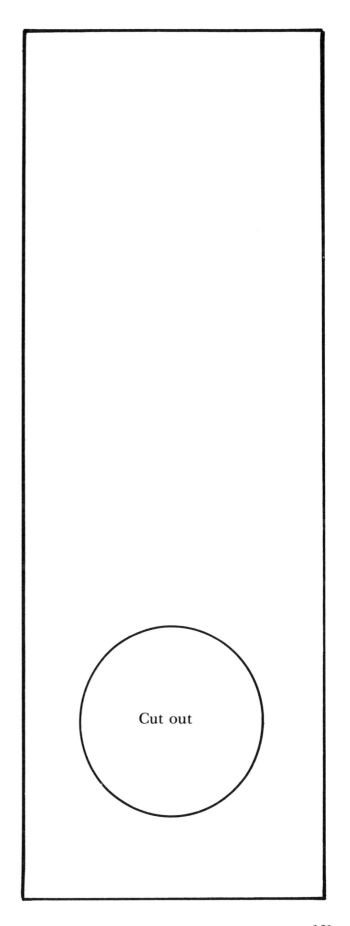

Cut out

Unit X
Animals

The farm animals in this unit are the cow, horse, pig, sheep, goat, and hen; and the zoo animals are the giraffe, zebra, elephant, camel, tiger (animals that walk) and the dolphin, porpoise, seal, and walrus (animals that swim). Other farm and zoo animals may be substituted or added.

Before beginning this unit and again after completing it, the children should visit a farm and a zoo to see the animals studied.

Language Development— Goals, Objectives, and Vocabulary

Goals

To establish a basic vocabulary foundation and to increase the ability to recall specific vocabulary

To improve categorization skills while increasing the ability to associate animals with their attributes, environment, and relationship to humans

Objectives

Receptive

The student will:

1. Recognize farm and zoo animals

2. Associate the characteristics of a farm with its functions

3. Identify animals that live on a farm

4. Identify parts of each farm animal when named

5. Match baby farm animals to adult farm animals

6. Associate farm animals with their products

7. Recognize characteristics and parts of zoo animals

8. Recognize zoo animals and their physical attributes

9. Identify zoo animals that live in the water

10. Associate each farm and zoo animal with its movement

Expressive

The student will:

1. Name farm and zoo animals

2. Contrast similarities and differences between farm and zoo animals

3. Name parts of each farm animal upon request

4. Name farm animals and their babies

5. Identify farm animals in a part-to-whole activity

6. Name zoo animals when presented with a picture

7. Describe characteristics of zoo animals

8. Compare similarities and differences of zoo animals that swim

Vocabulary

farm	elephant	farmhouse	jungle
cow	camel	barn	desert
horse	tiger	calf	tusks
pig	dolphin	colt	flippers
sheep	porpoise	piglet	fur
goat	seal	lamb	whiskers
hen	walrus	kid	snout
zoo	farmer	chick	short
giraffe	field	plains	long

Lesson 1—*(Introductory)*
Farm Animals

Objective—To identify and label farm animals

Materials—

Farm Scene (See preparation instructions below)

Shoebox

Farm Animals pictures
   (See preparation instructions below)

Scissors

Construction paper

Paste

Thumbtacks and bulletin board (optional)

Preparing the materials—Reproduce the Farm Scene (page 173) and the Farm Animals pictures (pages 174-175). Cut apart the pictures. Color each one and mount it on construction paper.

Procedure—

1. "Today we are going to talk about farms. We'll learn the names of some of the animals that live on the farm and the name of a farm building." Show the picture of the farm and discuss its features. If the children have visited a farm, help them recall what they saw. Discuss general information about farms: Much of the food we eat is grown on farms, we get meat and milk and eggs from farm animals, the farmer takes care of the animals on the farm by feeding them and giving them a clean place to live.

Teach the children the word *barn*. Explain that it is a "house" for the animals and that their food is stored there.

2. Place the shoebox on the table. "In this box I have pictures of some farm animals." One at a time, place the pictures of the cow, the horse, the pig, the sheep, the goat, and the hen, on the table. As each is shown, ask, "Does anyone know the name of this farm animal? Yes, this is a _____ ." Have the children repeat the sentence.

3. Name an animal and ask a child to place the picture of that animal back in the box. Give each child several opportunities. "Joe, will you put the (cow) in the box? Kathy, what animal did he place in the box?" Continue until all animals have been returned to the box.

4. Tack the farm animal pictures lightly onto a bulletin board (or place the pictures face up on the table). In turn, ask each child to point to the picture of the animal you name. "Joe, point to the picture of the pig."

5. Give each child a farm animal picture. Ask the child to hold the picture so the other children can see it. "I will come around to each of you, point to your picture, and ask, 'What is this?' Tell us what it is by saying, 'This is a _____.'" After the child responds, collect the picture.

Lesson 2—*(Introductory)*
Farm Animal Parts

Objective—To point to the mouth, head, tail, legs, and eyes of specified farm animals

Materials—Farm Animals pictures (from Lesson 1)

Procedure—

1. "Let's begin today by remembering the names of the animals we learned yesterday." Have the children recall as many animal names as they can. "Let's see if we forgot any. I'll show you a picture, and you tell us what it is by saying 'This is a _____!'" Demonstrate and then show the cow, goat, horse, sheep, hen, and pig.

2. "We'll look at each of the pictures again, but this time we'll look to see what kinds of body parts the animals have." Show the cow. Point to one of the cow's legs. "On what part of the cow is my finger? Yes, it's on one of the cow's legs" (or inform the children, "This is one of the cow's legs"). "People have legs, also. Touch your leg. How many legs do we have? How many legs do cows have?"

3. "Do these other farm animals have legs? Let's see." Place the farm animal pictures in a row on the table and give each child a turn to respond.

    a. "Does the sheep have legs? Point to one of the sheep's legs. How many legs does the sheep have?"

    b. "Does the goat have legs? Point to one of the goat's legs. How many legs does the goat have?"

    c. "Does the hen have legs? Point to one of the hen's legs. How many legs does the hen have?"

    d. "Does the horse have legs? Point to one of the horse's legs. How many legs does the horse have?"

    e. "Does the pig have legs? Point to one of the pig's legs. How many legs does the pig have?"

4. Review. "Did all these farm animals have legs? Did the cow have legs? Did the sheep have legs? Did the goat have legs? Did the hen have legs? Did the horse have legs? Did the pig have legs? Yes, all these animals had legs."

5. Discuss other body parts (head, mouth, eyes, and tail) in the same manner.

    a. "Point to the cow's _____."

    b. "What part of the cow's body is this?"

    c. "Do people have _____?"

    d. "Put your finger on your _____."

    e. "How many _____ do we have?"

    f. "How many _____ does the cow have?"

    g. "Do these other farm animals have _____? Let's see."

    h. "Does the _____ have _____? Point to its _____. How many _____ does it have?"

    Repeat this pattern for each farm animal picture. Review. "Did all these animals have _____?" Repeat for each farm animal represented. "Yes, all these animals had _____."

6. "Now we're ready to play a game. We know that all these animals had tails and heads and legs and eyes and mouths. Joe, put your finger on the cow's mouth. Lisa, put your finger on the pig's tail." Continue to give directions involving different animals and different body parts until the children respond correctly and quickly.

Lesson 3—(Introductory)
Baby Farm Animals

Objective—To pair the pictures of mother farm animals with their babies

Materials—

Farm Animals pictures (from Lesson 1)
Baby Farm Animals pictures
   (See preparation instructions below)
Scissors
Paste
Construction paper

Preparing the materials—Reproduce the Baby Farm Animals pictures (pages 176-177). Cut apart the pictures. Color each one and mount it on construction paper.

Procedure—

1. "Today we are going to learn the names of some baby farm animals. Did you know that all the animals we have talked about have babies? I'll show you pictures of some baby animals and pictures of their mothers. You already know the names of the mother animals, but each of the babies has a different name that you'll learn today."

2. Show the following pictures in pairs:

    a. Cow and calf
    b. Horse and colt
    c. Pig and piglet
    d. Sheep and lamb
    e. Goat and kid
    f. Hen and chick

   As each pair is shown, explain: "This is a _____ (adult animal's name) and this is its baby. The baby is called a _____ ."
   Have the children repeat the name of the baby.

3. Present each pair again and follow this procedure:

    a. Present the picture of each adult animal beside the picture of its baby.
    b. Point to the baby animal.
    c. Say, "This is a picture of a baby cow. A baby cow is called a _____ . Let's all say that: A baby cow is called a _____. Let's say it again. A baby cow is called a _____ ."

4. Place all the mother–baby pairs on the table and review the names of the babies by pointing to each and asking what it is called. Continue until each baby has been named twice.

5. With the paired pictures on the table, randomly point to either an adult or a baby and ask, "What is the name of this animal?" If you are pointing to, for example, a colt and the child responds "horse," say, "Yes, that's a horse, but it's a baby horse. What is a baby horse called?"

6. Give each child a picture of a baby animal. Place the pictures of the adult animals on your lap. "I'll hold up a picture of an animal. If you have that animal's baby, hold it up so we can see it."

    a. Hold up the goat. "Who has the baby for this animal? What is a baby goat called?"
    b. Continue, holding up each adult animal picture and asking, "Who has the baby for this animal? What is a baby _____ called?"
    c. Mix the adult farm animal pictures and ask the children to exchange baby farm animal pictures. Repeat until the children respond quickly and accurately.

7. Place the adult farm animal pictures on the table. "Find the mother for the baby animal you have. Put the baby on top of its mother." Collect the paired pictures.

Lesson 4—_(Reinforcement)_
Farm Animal Faces

Objective—To identify a farm animal when shown only its head

Materials—

Farm Animals pictures (from Lesson 1)
Barn (See preparation instructions below)
Construction paper
Scissors

Preparing the materials—Reproduce the barn (page 178) on construction paper. Cut a slit in the barn door, following the dotted line. (Do _not_ cut around three sides of the barn doors; cut _only_ a slit. The barn doors will not be opened. The animal pictures will be inserted in the slit to reveal a portion of the animal.)

Procedure—

1. Place the farm animal pictures in a row on the table. Have the children identify each by name.

2. Review the body parts learned in Lesson 2 (tail, legs, head, eyes, mouth). "Juan, put your finger on the cow's tail." Vary the animals and the body parts in these directions and give each child two or three turns.

3. Show the construction-paper barn. "This is a paper barn I've made. We're going to play a game called Guess What's Hiding in the Barn! I'll show you _part_ of an animal. The rest of the animal will be hidden in the barn. You look at part of the animal and guess which animal is in the barn."

4. Place all the animal pictures on your lap. Instruct the children to close their eyes. Place the horse in the barn so only its head is visible.

5. "Open your eyes. What animal is hidden in the barn?" After the children have guessed correctly or fail to make a correct guess after several attempts, show them the complete horse picture and state the conclusion. "A horse was hiding in the barn."

6. Continue to hide all but the heads of the other animals and play the game as described above.

7. Play the game a second time, hiding all but the _tail_ of each animal.

8. Play the game a third time, sometimes showing the head and sometimes the tail.

Lesson 5—_(Extension)_
Farm Animal Products

Objective—To identify products from farm animals

Materials—

Farm Animals pictures (from Lesson 1)
Animal Products pictures
    (See preparation instructions below)
Farm Animal Products Worksheet
    (See preparation instructions below)
Scissors
Construction paper
Paste

Preparing the materials—

1. Reproduce the Animal Products pictures (pages 179-180). Color each picture and mount it on construction paper.

2. Reproduce the Farm Animal Products Worksheet (page 181). Make a copy for each child.

Procedure—

1. "Did you know we get many kinds of food and clothing from the farm animals we've talked about? Today we'll learn about some of the things farm animals give us."

2. Place the cow, pig, hen, and sheep pictures in a row on the table. "These are the animals we'll talk about—the cow, the pig, the hen, and the sheep."

3. "Look at this picture." Show the picture of milk. "What is it? Does anyone know which animal gives us milk?" Explain that the cow gives us the milk we drink. "The cow gives us milk, so we'll put the picture of milk under the picture of the cow."

4. Discuss the other products in the same way.

    a. "Look at this picture."
    b. "What is it?"

c. "Does anyone know from which animal we get it?" When you show the picture of the sweater, ask, "Does anyone know which animal gives us wool to make sweaters?"

d. If the children do not know from which animal a given product comes, inform them.

e. "We get _(product)_ from the _(animal)_, so we'll put the picture of the _(product)_ under the picture of the _(animal)_.

5. While the paired pictures remain on the table, point to the appropriate pictures and review:

a. "We get milk for cheese from the _(cow)_."

b. "We get hamburger from the _(cow)_."

c. "We get bacon from the _(pig)_."

d. "We get eggs from the _(hen)_."

e. "We get fried chicken from the _(hen)_."

f. "We get milk for yogurt from the _(cow)_."

g. "We get wool for sweaters from the _(sheep)_."

6. Leave the paired pictures on the table and ask the children the following questions:

a. "From which animal do we get eggs?"

b. "From which animal do we get wool for sweaters?"

c. "From which animal do we get bacon?"

d. "From which animal do we get fried chicken?"

e. "From which animal do we get milk?"

f. "From which animal do we get hamburger?"

g. "From which animal do we get milk for cheese?"

7. Remove all pictures. Ask the questions listed in Step 6 again but in a different order. Provide no picture clues.

8. Give each child a Farm Animal Products Worksheet. Have the children name the items pictured (milk, eggs, bacon, mittens). Give each child at least one turn to tell from which animal a product comes. Repeat the series so each child has an opportunity to identify more than one animal with its product. Conclude with a review. "Put your finger on the picture that shows what we get from sheep . . . Put your finger on the picture that shows what we get from cows . . . Put your finger on the picture that shows what we get from pigs . . . Put your finger on the picture that shows what we get from hens."

Lesson 6—(Introductory) Zoo Animals that Walk

Objective—To identify zoo animals

Materials—

Picture of a zoo
(See preparation instructions below)
Pictures of Zoo Animals that Walk
(See preparation instructions below)
Scissors
Construction paper
Paste

Preparing the materials—Reproduce the picture of a zoo (page 182) and the pictures of Zoo Animals that Walk (pages 183-185). Cut apart the pictures. Color each picture and mount it on construction paper.

Procedure—

1. Show the class the picture of the zoo. Discuss the picture. Explain that a zoo is a place where many wild animals are kept. "These animals do not live on a farm like the cow and the pig and the other animals we've studied. Most of them used to live far away from here on plains with tall grass or in jungles with lots of trees or in deserts with sand. They weren't around people like the farm animals were. Now they have to be kept in special enclosures so they won't hurt people or run away." Discuss wild animals the children might have seen on current television shows that present the animals in their natural surroundings.

2. "Today we're going to learn the names of some of the animals that are kept in the zoo."

a. Show the picture of the giraffe. Point out to the class that a giraffe is the tallest animal in the zoo. "It has a very long neck, and it is yellow with dark brown marks. Who remembers the name of this animal? Yes, this is a giraffe. Where is this animal kept? Yes, it is kept in the zoo."

b. Show the picture of the zebra. Point out to the class that a zebra looks very much like a horse except for the black and white stripes all over its body. "What is this animal's name? Where is the zebra kept?"

c. Show the picture of the elephant. Point out to the class that an elephant is the largest animal in the zoo. It has a big trunk in front that it uses to put food into its mouth. It also has two long white tusks. "What is this animal's name? Yes, this is an elephant. Where is it kept?"

d. Show the picture of the camel. Point out that the camel is very tall. It has one or two humps on its back. "Who remembers this animal's name? Yes, it is a camel. Where do we keep it?"

e. Show the picture of the tiger. Point out that the tiger looks somewhat like a cat but that it is much larger and faster. It is yellow with black stripes. "What is its name? Yes, it is a tiger. Where is the tiger kept?"

3. Review each zoo animal by holding up its picture and asking, "What is the name of this animal? Where do we keep it? What do we know about this animal?"

4. Review the animal names again by holding up each picture and asking, "What is the name of this animal?"

Lesson 7—(Introductory)
Describing Zoo Animals that Walk

Objective—To describe zoo animals

Materials—

Set of miniature zoo animals—giraffe, zebra, elephant, camel, tiger (When selecting a set of miniature zoo animals, be sure the animals are sized in relation to one another. They should be realistic in appearance and appropriately painted or colored.)

Chalk and chalkboard

Box containing all the miniature zoo animals

Shoebox

Procedure—

1. "If you wanted to go outside, how would you get there? What part of your body would you use? Yes, people move about by using their legs and walking. The farm animals we studied also move about by walking. Remember how we pointed to their legs? The zoo animals we talked about yesterday also move about (travel) by walking."

2. "Think hard and let's see how many of those zoo animals we can name." As the children recall the names, write them on the chalkboard. Give clues, if necessary, to help the children recall the five animals.

3. Read back the list. Show each miniature zoo animal as its name is read and ask, "Does a _____ have legs? Does a _____ move about by walking?"

4. Briefly discuss each animal by asking the children to tell everything they know about the animal. They can discuss its size and color, how it moves, and its distinguishing characteristics.

5. Place the miniature animals back in the box. Place the shoebox on the table. "I'll ask you to close your eyes while Anita and I choose one of the animals in this box and put it in the shoebox. Then Anita will tell you about the animal in the shoebox and you will have to guess the animal's name. Ready? Close your eyes!" If necessary, help the child give the class clues without naming the animal. "This animal is kept in the zoo. It is yellow with brown marks. It has a very long neck." Have the child sit two or three feet from the group and peek at the animal from time to time to think of clues. When the class has identified the animal, return it to the assortment. Call on another child to act as the teacher. Continue to play until each child has had two turns to provide descriptive clues.

Conduct an additional lesson in which the children are blindfolded and attempt to identify the five miniature animals by touch. This lesson will help to emphasize certain distinguishing characteristics such as the camel's hump and the elephant's trunk or tusks.

Lesson 8—(Introductory)
Zoo Animals that Swim

Objective—To identify the dolphin, porpoise, seal, walrus

Materials—
Pictures of Zoo Animals that Swim
  (See preparation instructions below)
Scissors
Construction paper
Paste

Preparing the materials—Reproduce the pictures of Zoo Animals that Swim (pages 186-187). Cut apart the pictures. Color each picture and mount it on construction paper.

Procedure

1. "So far we've talked only about zoo animals that move about by walking. But there are many, many other kinds of zoo animals. Some of the animals are birds and can fly. Some of the animals live in the water and move around by swimming. Today we'll talk about some that live in the water."

2. Hold the picture of the seal in one hand and the picture of the walrus in the other. Ask the class to look closely at both pictures to see if they are the same. Allow the class time to compare the two animals and to look for similarities and differences. When a child points out a difference, confirm or correct the child's statement. If the class misses the main difference, point out that the seal has long whiskers around its mouth and fur or hair covering its body. A walrus looks similar to the seal, but it is larger. It has two long white tusks but no fur and no long whiskers. Discuss the flippers on each animal. Explain that the flippers are used in swimming and that both of these animals spend most of their time in water. Also explain that although these animals have no legs, they can walk by using their flippers. They can live in the water and out of the water. They move much faster in the water than out of it.

3. Repeat the names of the two animals. "The animal with the tusks is a walrus." Have the children repeat the word. "The animal with the long whiskers is a seal." Have the children repeat the word.

4. Show the picture of the seal again and ask, "What animal is this? Yes, this is a seal. How do you know that it is a seal? Yes, because it has long whiskers and a body covered with fur." Show each child the seal picture and ask for individual answers. "What is this? How do you know that this is a seal? How does a seal move around? Can a seal move around on land?"

5. Show the picture of the walrus again, and ask, "What is this? Yes, this is a walrus. How do you know that it is a walrus? Yes, because it has two long white tusks coming from its mouth. It has no fur and no long whiskers. It is larger than the seal we just saw, isn't it?" Show each child the walrus picture and ask for individual answers. "What is this? How do you know it's a walrus? How does a walrus move around?"

6. Hold the two pictures behind your back. Tell the class that you want them to tell you the name of the animal that you show. Mix the order in which the cards are presented so there is not a simple alternation. Ask each child in turn to identify the picture you show. Continue until all children respond quickly and correctly to each picture. Correct errors by asking the child to look for distinguishing characteristics.

7. Hold the picture of the dolphin in one hand and the picture of the porpoise in the other. Ask the class to look closely at both pictures. Allow them time to compare the two animals and to look for similarities and differences. When a child points out a difference, confirm or correct the child's statement. If the class misses the main differences, point out that a dolphin has a long, sharp nose or snout and a porpoise has a short, blunt snout. Point out that this is the main difference to be seen by looking at the pictures. "Do these animals have legs? Do these animals have flippers like the seal and walrus? Do you suppose they can walk? No, these animals never come out on land. They cannot walk. They can only swim."

8. Tell the children the names of the two animals. "The animal with the long sharp nose is a dolphin." Have the children repeat the word. "This animal with the short nose is a porpoise." Have the children repeat the word.

9. Show the picture of the dolphin again and ask, "What is this? Yes, this is a dolphin. How do you know that it's a dolphin? Yes, because it has a long sharp nose or snout." Show each child the dolphin picture and ask for individual answers. "What is this? How do you know that this is a dolphin? How does a dolphin move about?"

10. Show the picture of the porpoise again and ask, "What is this? Yes, this is a porpoise. How do you know that it is a porpoise? Yes, because it has a short nose or snout." Show each child the porpoise picture and ask for individual answers. "What is this? How do you know that this is a porpoise? How does the porpoise move about?"

11. Hold the two pictures behind your back. Tell the class that you want them to tell you the name of the animal you show. Show the first child the picture of the dolphin and ask, "What is this?" Put both pictures behind your back again. Show the next child the picture of the porpoise. Mix the order in which you show the pictures so there is not a simple alternation. Continue until the children identify the pictures quickly and correctly. If the child has difficulty, review the distinguishing characteristic.

12. Stack the pictures of the walrus, seal, dolphin, and porpoise. Show them in random order one at a time as in Step 11. Continue this presentation until the children consistently identify the four animals.

A similar lesson can be done in which the children learn the names of several zoo birds and their differences and similarities.

Lesson 9—*(Reinforcement)* Moving Like Zoo Animals

If a lesson on zoo birds was done, add bird pictures to the pictures of zoo animals included in this lesson.

Objective—To move like a zoo animal

Materials—

Pictures of Zoo Animals that Walk (from Lesson 6)
Pictures of Zoo Animals that Swim (from Lesson 8)

Procedure—

1. "We have studied two kinds of zoo animals—those that travel by walking and those that travel by swimming."

2. "Let's see how many zoo animals you can name that travel by walking." Have the children recall the tiger, zebra, giraffe, elephant, and camel. As they recall an animal, hold up its picture and say, "Yes, the _____ has legs and it travels by walking."

3. Using a similar procedure, help the children recall the zoo animals that travel by swimming (porpoise, dolphin, seal, walrus).

4. Place both sets of animal pictures randomly on the table. Have the children take turns following these directions:

   a. Take a picture of an animal that travels by walking.

   b. Take a picture of an animal that travels by swimming.

   c. Continue to repeat these two requests in varied order until all pictures have been taken.

5. Say to each child, in turn, "Tell us the name of your animal. Now pretend you are that animal. Show us how you would travel." Help the child imitate the animal walking or swimming. When each child has had a turn, collect the pictures.

6. Have all the children stand in a line in the center of the room. "I'll hold up a picture of an animal. When you know what it is, don't say anything, just show me how it travels. Pretend to walk or to swim like that animal." Hold up the pictures one by one and have the children move appropriately.

Lesson 10—(Extension)
Farm and Zoo Animals

Objective—To tell how farm and zoo animals are alike and different

Materials—

Farm Animals pictures (from Lesson 1)
Pictures of Zoo Animals that Walk (from Lesson 6)

Procedure—

1. Show the cow and horse pictures. "Look at these two pictures. How are they the same?" Help the children to identify similarities *(both are animals, both have legs, both have heads, both are farm animals, . . .)*. Restate the similarities named.

2. Show the giraffe and camel pictures. "Look at these two pictures. How are these two the same?" Help the children to identify similarities *(both are animals, both are kept at the zoo, both have tails, both have eyes, . . .)*.

3. In the same manner, ask the children to identify similarities in the following picture pairs:

    a. Pig and zebra
    b. Sheep and tiger
    c. Goat and elephant
    d. Hen and giraffe
    e. Cow and camel

4. Show each picture pair again, but ask the children to tell how the two animals are different. "You've thought of ways in which these animals are the same. I'll show you the pictures again, and this time I want you to tell me how the animals are different."

    a. Show the cow and horse. "How are these two different?" It may be necessary to give the children examples of differences *(they are different colors, they have different names—one is a cow and the other is a horse, . . .)*. When possible, ask questions to help the children deduce differences rather than merely telling them differences.

    b. Show the remaining pairs and ask the children to describe differences in the giraffe and camel, pig and zebra, sheep and tiger, goat and elephant, hen and giraffe, cow and camel.

Farm Scene

Farm Animals

174

Farm Animals

Baby Farm Animals

176

Baby Farm Animals

Guess What's Hiding in the Barn!

Animal Products

Animal Products

Farm Animal Products Worksheet

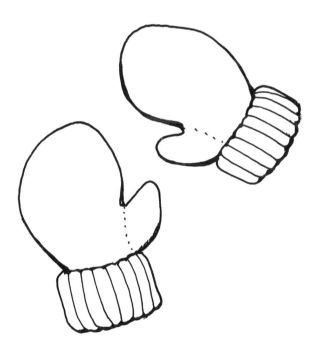

The Zoo

Zoo Animals that Walk

Zoo Animals that Walk

Zoo Animals that Swim

Zoo Animals that Swim

187

Unit XI
Weather and Seasons

Time and seasons are difficult concepts for preschoolers. They develop understanding of these concepts through day-to-day observation of changes. The ideas presented particularly in Lessons 1 through 5 should be reinforced and expanded frequently through informal observations and discussions with the children—at lunchtime, when walking to and from the bus, and on rainy or snowy days.

This unit is designed for areas with cold winters and hot summers. The materials can be changed to adapt to areas with different climates.

Language Development—
Goals, Objectives, and Vocabulary

Goals

To increase the recognition and understanding of the concepts involved in time and seasons

To become aware of the changes that occur in weather, activities, and clothing during each season

Objectives

Receptive

The student will:

1. Comprehend the concept of four seasons

2. Comprehend and recognize the different attributes of each season

3. Classify attributes of each season including weather, clothing worn, and activities

4. Compare the similarities and differences of each season including weather, clothing, and activities

5. Compare and describe physical characteristics of various tree leaves

6. Match trees in various stages to the appropriate season

7. Match the correct clothing to the appropriate season

8. Match sports and other activities to the appropriate season

9. Identify various types of weather by pointing to the correct picture when named

10. Comprehend the meaning of *steam* and *cloud* and associate water with steam and clouds

Expressive

The student will:

1. Name the four seasons when presented with appropriate pictures of each

2. Describe the type of weather that is happening on any given day and in pictures

3. Model days of the week

4. Name the month, day, and weather on a daily basis in a group activity

Vocabulary

rainy	spring	grass	warm	heavy	clouds
snowy	blossoms	bloom	warmer	cooler	evaporate
seasons	buds	snow	hats	snow	calendar
summer	weather	colder	mittens	wet	day
fall	sweaters	coldest	light	dry	months
winter	jackets				

Lesson 1—*(Introductory)* Seasons

This lesson should be done on a cool fall day when the leaves have started to turn color and fall from the trees.

Objective—To identify the seasons

Materials—Pictures of Trees
(See preparation instructions below)

Preparing the materials—Reproduce the pictures of trees (pages 200-203). Color each picture.

Procedure

1. "The year is divided into four parts. The four parts are called seasons. Each season has a name. The names of the seasons are summer, fall, winter, and spring.

2. "Summer has just ended and the season now is fall. In fall children go back to school. Are your brothers and sisters going to school now? In fall it starts to get cooler, and we need to wear jackets or sweaters outside. Did anyone wear a coat or a sweater or a jacket to school today? In fall the leaves on many trees begin to turn color and fall off the trees." Have the children look out the window to observe the colors of the leaves and the leaves on the ground.

Show the picture of the fall tree. "Here is a picture of a tree in fall. How can we tell it is fall? Yes, the leaves are red and gold and brown; only a few green leaves are left. Some of the leaves are falling off the trees."

3. "As the year goes on, it becomes colder and colder and more leaves fall off the trees until many trees have no leaves at all. Fall will turn into winter and we'll need to wear warmer clothes. We'll need heavy coats and hats and gloves to go outside. Winter is the coldest time of the year. It often snows in the winter."

Show the picture of the winter tree. "Here is a picture of a tree in winter. How can we tell it is winter? Yes, there are no leaves on the tree, and there is snow on the ground."

Review. "Which two seasons have we talked about so far? Which season is it now?"

4. "After winter comes a season called spring. Slowly the weather gets warmer again and the trees begin to get new leaves. We begin wearing jackets and sweaters again in the spring. We don't need our big heavy coats and hats and mittens any more because it isn't cold enough. The grass gets green and flowers bloom in the spring."

Show the picture of the spring tree. "Here is a picture of a tree in spring. How can we tell it is spring? Yes, there are little buds on the tree and blossoms. The tree is putting out new leaves on its branches and the grass is green again."

5. "As spring goes on, it gets warmer and warmer and spring turns into summer. By summer, the trees have lots of leaves. It is so hot outside that we don't wear coats and jackets. We wear very light clothes. Sometimes we go swimming."

Show the picture of the summer tree. "Here is a picture of a tree in summer. How can we tell it is summer? Yes, the tree has lots of leaves on it and the grass is very green."

"As the summer goes on, it begins to get cooler until it is fall again, like now."

6. Review. "What are the names of the seasons?" Show the four pictures again and quickly review the characteristics of the trees during each of the four seasons.

Present Lesson 11 soon after this lesson.

Lesson 2—(Introductory) Fall

This lesson should be done on the day after Lesson 1 or on the next typical cool fall day.

Objective—To identify the fall season

Materials—

Lined newsprint
Marking pen
Camera (preferably Polaroid) and color film
Crayons—one for each child

Procedure—

1. "Yesterday we talked about the four seasons of the year. What were the names of the seasons?"

   "Today we'll talk more about one season. Who remembers the name of the season it is now? Yes, it's fall." Help the children to talk about fall by asking about the clothes they wear, what they do, how the trees look, how the grass looks, . . . Print their comments in sentence form on lined newsprint. Explain to the children that you are writing their answers so they can be read later in the year. Read back the story.

2. Take the children on a walk outside. Ask each child to find three or four leaves that have fallen off the trees. Discuss the colors. How do those leaves feel compared to green leaves still on the trees? Have the children keep the fallen leaves to be used later.

3. Take a picture of the children standing beside a fall tree. Explain that as the seasons change, you will take their picture again beside this same tree. They will see how the tree changes as the seasons change. Take their picture beside an evergreen tree and explain that this tree will not change very much. It is called an evergreen and stays green through all the seasons.

4. Return to the classroom. Show the children how to make leaf prints. Place a leaf on the table and place a piece of newsprint on top of it. Rub back and forth over the paper above the leaf with the side of a crayon. Help each child make several leaf prints.

5. When the photographs have been developed, attach them to the printed comments the children made about fall. A fall display can be made on the bulletin board by using the photographs, the story, and the leaf prints made by the children. Save the photographs and the fall story for later lessons.

Present Lesson 6 soon after this lesson.

Lesson 3—(Introductory) Winter

This lesson should be done on a typical cold winter day when it is not snowing.

Objective—To identify the winter season

Materials—

Fall photographs and story from Lesson 2.
Camera (preferably Polaroid) and color film
Lined newsprint
Marking pen

Procedure—

1. "We haven't talked about the seasons for a while. Did you know it's a different season now? Remember, when school began it was fall? What did the trees look like in fall?" Show the children the photographs and read the story from the fall lesson. "Is it still fall? No. The season changed. It has gotten much colder. The name of the season now is winter."

2. "We wrote a fall story. Now let's write a winter story. Then when the season changes again, we'll be able to remember what winter was like." Help the children to talk about winter by asking about the clothes they wear, what they do, how the trees look, how the grass looks, . . . Print their comments in sentence form on the lined newsprint. Read back the story.

3. Take the children outside. Take their photograph standing in front of the same tree that was used for the fall picture. Discuss the cold, their clothes, and the trees. Take their photograph in front of the evergreen. Note that it is still green. Return to the classroom.

4. When the film is developed, attach the photographs to the winter story and display it on a bulletin board next to the fall photographs and story. Compare the photographs, and note that the evergreen has remained the same while the other tree has lost all its leaves. Save the photographs and stories for later lessons.

Present Lesson 7 soon after this lesson.

Lesson 4—*(Introductory)* Spring

This lesson should be done on a typical warm spring day when the buds are evident on the trees.

Objective—To identify the spring season

Materials—

Fall photographs and story from Lesson 2
Winter photographs and story from Lesson 3
Camera (preferably Polaroid) and color film
Lined newsprint
Marking pen

Procedure—

1. Show the fall photographs and story. "Remember when we took this picture and wrote this story? What season was it?" Read the story. "Is it fall now?"

2. Show the winter photographs and story. "Remember when we took this picture and wrote this story? What season was it?" Read the story. "Is it winter now? No, the season has changed again. When we first came to school it was fall. Then it got very cold and it was winter. Now the season has changed again. It has gotten warmer, and it's spring now."

3. "Let's write a spring story." Help the children talk about spring by asking about the clothes they wear, what they do, how the trees look, how the grass looks, . . . Print their comments in sentence form on the lined newsprint. Read back the story.

4. Take the children outside. Take their photograph standing in front of the same two trees that were used for the fall and winter photographs. Discuss their clothes, the trees, what people are doing. Return to the classroom.

5. When the film is developed, attach the photographs to the story and display it on a bulletin board beside the fall and winter photographs and stories. Compare the trees in the three sets of photographs. Although it appears that the evergreen has not changed, point out to the children that it does have some buds and new growth. Save the photographs and stories for later lessons.

Lesson 5—*(Introductory)* Summer

If school is held in summer, do a lesson similar to Lessons 2, 3, and 4. If school ends in May or early June, do the following lesson near the end of spring when the trees are full with leaves.

Objective—To choose a picture of a person dressed in summer clothes

Materials—

Pictures of People in Spring
  (See preparation instructions below)
Pictures of People in Summer
  (See preparation instructions below)
Fall photographs and story from Lesson 2
Winter photographs and story from Lesson 3
Spring photographs and story from Lesson 4
Lined newsprint
Marking pen

Preparing the materials—Reproduce the pictures of people in spring (pages 204-205) and in summer (pages 206-207). Color the pictures.

Procedure—

1. "So far we've talked about three seasons." Show the photographs and read the stories for fall, winter, and spring. "What season is it now? Yes, spring. When school is over for the year, it will be summer. Since we won't be here during the summer to talk about it, we'll talk about it now."

   "It's warm outside now. We need only light jackets or sweaters when we go outside. We don't wear heavy coats the way we did in winter. Soon it will get so warm outside that we won't wear jackets or sweaters any more. It may even be too hot to wear the kinds of clothes we're wearing now. We may want to wear shorts instead of long pants or dresses, and we'll wear shirts or dresses without sleeves. Sometimes we may go swimming to get cool."

2. "Here are pictures of people. Some of the people are dressed for spring. Some of the people are dressed for summer. Let's look at the pictures and decide which people are dressed for summer and which are dressed for spring."

   Discuss each picture with the children in terms of the clothes worn by the people and the activities the people are involved in. As the pictures are discussed, sort them into two piles (people dressed for summer, people dressed for spring).

   Remove the summer pictures. Spread the spring pictures on the table. "We said these people were all dressed for *(spring)*. What kinds of clothes are they wearing? What kinds of things are they doing?"

3. Follow the same procedure with the summer pictures.

4. Summarize by writing a summer story, using the children's ideas as in the other season stories. Read back the story.

Lesson 6—*(Reinforcement)* Leaves

This lesson should be done on the day after Lesson 2 or the next typical cool fall day.

Objective—To describe distinguishing characteristics of different types of leaves

Materials—
Sewing needles (with eyes large enough for string) —one for each child
String

Procedure—

1. "Yesterday we went outside and found some leaves and used them to make pictures. Today we'll go outside again to find leaves. We'll bring them inside and make leaf necklaces. Each of you, look closely and try to find as many different kinds of leaves as you can. There are many different kinds of trees, and each kind of tree has a different leaf. The leaves are many different colors, too, because it is fall and they are changing colors. Let's see how many different colors we can find."

2. Take the children outside and help them to locate a variety of leaves in different colors and sizes. Return to the classroom.

3. Ask the children to spread out their leaves on the table. Discuss the variety of leaves and the different colors, shapes, and sizes. Name the various leaves—oak, maple, sycamore.

4. Demonstrate how to make a leaf necklace by stringing leaves, using needle and string. Pass the needle through the thickest section of each leaf to avoid tearing. Tie the ends of the string together after several leaves are strung. Thread a needle for each child. Help the children to make their own leaf necklaces. Each necklace should have at least five leaves.

5. Let the children wear their necklaces. Comment on the different kinds of leaves. Ask the children to describe some of the distinguishing characteristics of the different types of leaves. *(Lots of points, big stem, star shape, . . .)*

Lesson 7—(Reinforcement) Snow

This lesson must be done on a snowy day. It should be done after Lesson 3.

Objective—To state facts about snow

Materials—Paper cup

Procedure—

1. "Look outside. What is all the white stuff you see? Yes, it's snow. Today we're going to go outside and learn some things about the snow. What is the name of the season? Yes, winter. Winter is the snowy season."

2. Have the children dress warmly. Take them outside. "What are some things we can do with the snow?" Have the children do whatever things are suggested. Be sure to include making footprints and handprints in the snow, making snowballs, making a snowman as a group, and melting some snow in your hand.

3. Fill the paper cup with snow. Return to the classroom. "Outside we saw snow melt when I held it in my hand. When it melted, it turned to _(water)_. Snow _is_ water, just like rain. But it's so cold outside that as the water comes from the clouds it begins to freeze and becomes snow instead of rain. Here is the cup of snow we got outside. It is warmer in our room than outside. What do you think will happen to the cup of snow in here? Yes, it will melt. When it has melted, it will be _(water)_. Snow is frozen water."

Place the cup aside. Later show the children the cup and observe the water. Discuss the fact that the snow was frozen water; when it melted, it changed back to water.

Lesson 8—(Reinforcement) Trees in Season

This lesson should be done in the springtime. It is a good indoor activity for a rainy day.

Objective—To match trees in the same season

Materials—

Pictures of Trees (from Lesson 1)

Spinner board
(See preparation instructions below)

Season words
(See preparation instructions below)

Individual Tree Pictures
(See preparation instructions below)

Preparing the materials—

1. a. In the center of a 36″ square of masonite, drill a hole large enough to insert a ¼″ nut and bolt.

b. Cut a 12″ x 2″ piece of masonite for a spinner. Drill a hole in the center large enough to insert the nut and bolt.

c. With cardboard or masonite, attach a point to the spinner. Place the ¼″ nut through the hole in the spinner, place two washers on the nut, place the nut through the hole in the board, and screw the bolt to the nut at the back of the board.

Assembled spinner board

2. Print the words FALL, WINTER, SPRING, SUMMER on four separate 8″ x 3″ pieces of construction paper.

3. Reproduce the individual tree pictures (page 208). Make one copy for each child. Cut out the individual pictures and mount each on construction paper.

Procedure—

1. "We've talked about the four seasons of the year. Let's name them. When we came to school, it was *(fall)*. Then it became very cold and sometimes it snowed; it was *(winter)*. It began to get warmer again, and the leaves started coming back on the trees; now it is *(spring)*. When school is over and it gets very hot outside, it will be *(summer)*. The four seasons are fall, winter, spring, and summer."

2. Hold up the picture of the tree in fall. "What season is it when the trees look like this? Yes, fall." Put the picture in the upper left corner of the spinner board. Show the word FALL. "This is a word. It tells us what season it is in the picture. What do you suppose this word says? Yes, this word says *fall.*" Attach the word to the board directly below the picture of the tree in fall. Discuss and place the winter, spring, and summer pictures of trees in the same way. Put the appropriate word labels beneath each picture. The winter tree goes in the upper right, the spring tree in the lower right, and the summer tree in the lower left.

3. Show the individual tree pictures. "I'm going to give each of you a small picture of a tree in each season." Have the children identify the season represented by each tree picture and explain how they know it is the season they named. Give each child a set of four pictures.

4. "Now we're ready to play a game. This is a spinner. You will take turns spinning it. (Demonstrate.) When the spinner stops, tell us the name of the season shown by the tree. Then find the tree picture you have that shows the same season and give it to me. The person who gets rid of all four pictures first wins the game." If the spinner stops on a season for which the child no longer has a picture, the child merely names the season and waits for another turn to try to match the remaining pictures. Continue until at least one child holds no pictures. If time permits, continue until all children are empty-handed.

Lesson 9—*(Extension)* Seasonal Clothes

This lesson should be done after Lesson 8.

Objective—To dress a paper doll in clothing appropriate for the different seasons

Materials—

Seasonal Clothing Cutouts
(See preparation instructions below)

Box containing at least 20 fabric samples including fur, wool, and cotton

Preparing the materials—Reproduce the Seasonal Clothing Cutouts (pages 209-213). Make a set for each child. Color the pictures. (You may want to use different colors to indicate whether clothing is for the boy or the girl doll.) Cut out the dolls and the clothing.

Procedure—

1. "Yesterday we played a spinner game about the seasons. We talked about how we can tell what season it is by the way the trees look. We can also tell what season it is by the way people dress."

2. Show the box of fabrics. "In the winter when it's very cold, we wear warm clothes made from warm, heavy fabrics. Look at these pieces of fabric and try to find things you think would be good to wear in the winter." Discuss the children's choices. Discuss whether the materials would be used for outer garments such as coats. Name the fabrics. Discuss fabrics which might be used to make clothes for other seasons.

3. Show one set of cutouts. "Here are some children and some clothes. We'll dress them for the different seasons. Let's begin with winter.

What would they wear in the winter?" Let the children choose and discuss their choices. "Why do you think they'd wear that? Yes, because in the winter it is very cold outside and they would need heavy coats or jackets." Have the children choose and explain their choices for summer, fall, and spring. Discuss why people wear the same clothes in fall and spring.

4. Give each child a set of cutouts. Have the children dress their dolls and discuss the results each time. "Dress the doll for winter . . . Dress the doll for spring . . . Dress the doll for summer . . . Dress the doll for fall . . . Dress the doll for summer . . . Dress the doll for winter . . . Dress the doll for spring . . . Dress the doll for fall."

Lesson 10—(Extension) Seasonal Activities

Objective—To identify the season associated with a particular activity or set of characteristics

Procedure—

1. "Today we'll play a guessing game. I'll tell you something we do or see, and you tell me what season I'm thinking of. Listen closely. I'm going to go swimming. What season would it be if I were going swimming? Yes, it would be summer."

2. Ask the children to identify the season in each of the following:

   "I'm going to rake the leaves that have fallen off the trees." *(fall)*

   "I'm going to pick some flowers." *(spring, summer, fall)*

   "I'm going to go ice skating." *(winter)*

   "I'm going to go to school for the first time after the summer vacation." *(fall)*

"I see little buds on the trees, but there aren't many leaves." *(spring)*

"I see lots of snow." *(winter)*

"I'm going to wear a sweater and go outside and jump rope." *(fall or spring)*

"It's so hot: I'm going to sit under a shady tree that has lots of leaves and drink something cold." *(summer)*

"I see people wearing heavy coats and gloves and hats." *(winter)*

"It's very, very cold outside." *(winter)*

"I see people wearing shorts." *(summer)*

"I see trees without any leaves." *(winter)*

"I see lots of green leaves on the trees, and the grass is very green." *(summer)*

"I see people wearing swimming suits." *(summer)*

Lesson 11—*(Introductory)*
Weather Words

This lesson should follow Lesson 1.

Objective—To identify a cloudy, sunny, rainy, or snowy day

Materials—Weather Pictures (See preparation instructions below)

Preparing the materials—Reproduce the weather pictures (pages 214-217). Mount them on construction paper.

Procedure—

1. "There are lots of words that tell us what kind of day it is. We've already talked about some of those words. In the winter the days are very cold; in the summer the days are very hot. Some days during the year are hot, some are warm, some are cool, and some are cold. What kind of day is it today?"

   "There are other words that tell us what kind of day it is. When the sun is shining, we say it is a *sunny* day. When the sun is covered by clouds and we can't see it shining, we say it is a *cloudy* day. When it's raining, we say it is a *rainy* day. When it's snowing, we say it is a *snowy* day."

2. "I have some pictures for you to look at. We'll look at each picture and try to decide if it's a sunny day, a cloudy day, a rainy day, or a snowy day."

   Show the picture of the sunny day. "What is the weather like in this picture?" Use the word *weather* as much as possible during the lesson to help the children learn the association between the descriptive vocabulary and the weather. "Is it sunny or cloudy or rainy or snowy? Yes, it's a sunny day. How do we know it's sunny? Yes, we see children playing outside without raincoats or umbrellas." Discuss other features of the picture that indicate the sun is shining.

3. Present the other pictures in this order: cloudy day, rainy day, snowy day, cloudy day, rainy day, sunny day, snowy day. For each, first show the picture and ask, "What is the weather like in this picture? Is it sunny or cloudy or rainy or snowy?" After the children have responded, ask, "How do we know it is _____ ?" Discuss features of the pictures that indicate what the weather is like.

   While discussing the pictures, inform the children that:

   a. It is cloudy on rainy and snowy days. Rain and snow come out of the clouds.

   b. Rain and snow are water. When it is cold enough, rain turns to snow.

   c. On cloudy days we can't see the sun in the sky because the clouds are in front of the sun, but the sun is there just the same.

   d. It is darker outside on cloudy days than on sunny days because the clouds don't let as much sunlight get through to us.

4. Take one child at a time from the group to a window at least five feet away. "Look out the window. What is the weather like today? Is it a sunny day, a cloudy day, a rainy day, or a snowy day?"

Lesson 12—*(Extension)* Clouds

Use this lesson after Lesson 11 to clarify the discussion in that lesson. This lesson should be done shortly after the lesson on evaporation (Unit III, Lesson 4).

Objective—To show an awareness of how clouds are formed

Materials—

Hot plate
Teakettle containing 2 cups of water
Damp sponge
Eye dropper
Bowl of water
Paper towel

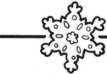

Procedure—

1. "Today we'll talk about clouds. You already know that clouds are made up of drops of water and that rain and snow come out of the clouds. I'll show you how the clouds are formed."

   Show the children the water in the teakettle. Heat the water until steam forms above the spout. "We can see steam coming out of the teakettle. What is the steam? Yes, it's water. As it comes out, it goes into the air. When water goes into the air, we say it evaporates. Water evaporates outside, too. Some of the rain that falls evaporates into the air. After a rain, the sidewalks are wet, but the heat from the sun makes the water on the sidewalk evaporate and go back into the air—just like the heat from our stove makes the water in the teakettle evaporate into the air. As more and more water evaporates, the drops of water group together and form clouds in the sky."

   Hold a paper towel in the cloud of steam. "If I hold a towel in this cloud of steam it gets wet. Why? Yes, because the cloud of steam is made up of little drops of water. The water goes into the towel and makes it wet."

   "Now, what have we learned so far?" Review. "We know water on the ground evaporates into the air. We also know the water drops go together and form clouds in the sky."

2. "Pretend we have lots of clouds in the sky now. Does the water ever come back to the ground from the clouds? Yes! It comes back down whenever it rains or snows. Watch, and I'll show you what happens." Show the sponge. "Let's pretend this sponge is a cloud. It's wet" (let the children feel it) "because the clouds are made up of (_water_). I'm going to put more and more water in this pretend cloud." As the children watch, use the eye dropper and the water from the dish to add water to the sponge. Hold the sponge above the table as you add the water. When the sponge is saturated with water, it will begin to drip. "What is happening? Yes, the water is coming out of the sponge. We could say our pretend cloud is raining. I put so much water in the sponge that it couldn't hold any more. Now some of the water is coming out and falling to the table. That's what happens to the clouds outside, too. When they have so much water in them that they can't hold any more, the water comes out of the clouds and falls to the ground as rain. If it's cold, the falling water freezes and turns to snow."

3. Review. "Pretend it has rained. The ground is all wet. Will it stay wet? No, it will dry. As the ground dries, where does the water go? Yes, it evaporates into the air. Then the water collects in the sky in (_clouds_). When the clouds get so full of water that they can't hold any more, what happens? Yes, it rains or snows, and the water returns to the ground."

Lesson 13—(Reinforcement) Weather Calendar

Objective—To match symbols to weather types

Materials—

   Calendar for Weather
   (See preparation instructions below)
   Newsprint
   Crayons

Preparing the materials—

1. On a 36-inch square of tagboard or cardboard, draw a calendar as shown. Each square is 5 inches.

Mark the month and the days of the week, but do not number the squares to show dates.

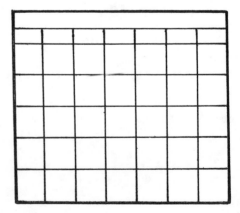

2. Reproduce a supply of weather indicator pictures (page 218). Cut them out, color them, and store them in envelopes near the calendar.

Procedure —

1. Show the calendar. "This is called a calendar. It helps us tell what day it is and what month it is. All the months of the year have names and all the days of the week have names. Each day, beginning today, we'll look at our calendar and talk about what month it is and what day it is. Then we'll decide what the weather is like, and we'll paste a picture on our calendar to show what the weather is like."

2. Point to the name of the month. "This word tells us the name of the month. The month is _____ . This word says _____ ." Have the children repeat the name of the month. Then ask, "What is the name of the month?"

3. Point to each of the days of the week. "These words tell us the names of the days in the week." Point to each word as you say, "This word says Monday, this word says Tuesday, . . . " and so on. "We come to school on Monday, Tuesday, Wednesday, Thursday, and Friday. We do not come to school on Saturday or Sunday. Today is _____ , so we will put our picture of the weather for today right here, under the word _____ . What is the name of the day today?"

4. Show the weather indicator pictures. Tell the children, "Every day, we are going to paste a picture on our calendar that shows what the weather is like that day. If we want to put a picture on our calendar to show what the weather is like today, which one of these should we use? What is the weather like today?" Point to the appropriate picture as you ask, "Is it sunny? Is it cloudy? Is it windy? Is it snowy? Is it rainy?"

It is possible that more than one indicator may be needed. For instance, it may be both rainy and windy. In that case, both pictures should be pasted on the calendar. If the children have difficulty deciding, have them look out the window or go outside to check the weather.

5. Continue to use and discuss the calendar each day for at least four weeks as a large-group activity or as a part of a small-group period. With each use:

   a. Label the calendar as a calendar.
   b. Name the month while pointing to the word, and then ask, "What is the name of the month?"
   c. Name the days while pointing to the words, then name the current day and ask, "What is the name of the day?"
   d. Discuss the weather of the day.
   e. Have the children decide which is the appropriate weather indicator and paste it on the calendar.

6. After the calendar has been used for at least four weeks, have each child select the appropriate weather indicator for a given day. Follow the procedure for a, b, and c outlined in Step 5. Then say, "Today I want Katie to decide all by herself which picture we should put on our calendar. We won't help her. Katie, look at the pictures and think about the weather today. Which of these pictures should you put on the calendar to show what the weather is like today?"

Individual calendars similar to the large calendar may be made for each child and maintained during the year. The children may paste appropriate weather symbols each day and take their calendars home at the end of each month.

Tree in Spring

200

Tree in Summer

Tree in Fall

Tree in Winter

People in Spring

People in Summer

Individual Tree Pictures

Seasonal Clothing Cutouts

Seasonal Clothing Cutouts

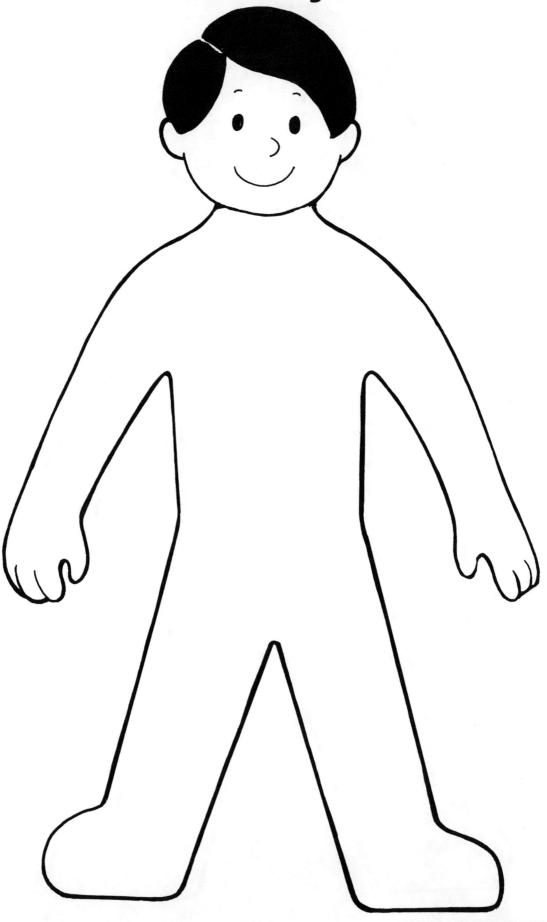

Seasonal Clothing Cutouts

Seasonal Clothing Cutouts

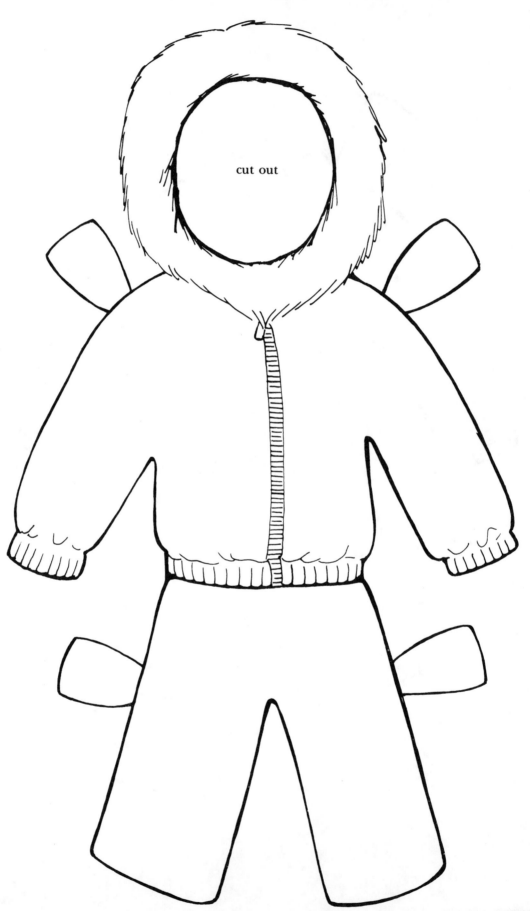

cut out

212

Seasonal Clothing Cutouts

Sunny Day

Cloudy Day

Rainy Day

Snowy Day

Weather Indicators

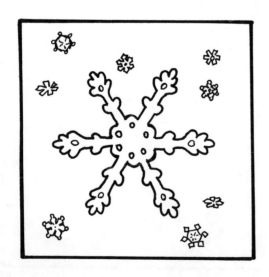

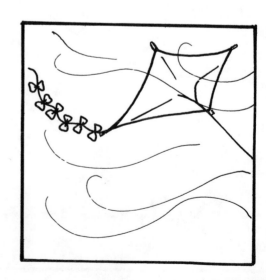

Unit XII
Magnetism

The lessons in this unit are designed around the use of horseshoe and bar magnets. The magnets must be strong enough to attract and hold the objects used in each lesson. Be sure to test the magnets before you begin.

In Lessons 1, 2, and 3, the children will test iron and noniron objects. Include some different objects for each lesson to sustain interest.

Items that will be attracted to a magnet include nails, needles, pins, screws, bolts, washers, bits of wire, a small horseshoe magnet, paper clips, tacks, hairpins, and small scissors.

Items that will not be attracted to a magnet include a wooden match, paper, toothpicks, wooden blocks, marbles, pebbles, wooden beads, crayons, a crumpled ball of tinfoil, and a pop bottle cap.

Language Development—
Goals, Objectives, and Vocabulary

Goals

To increase vocabulary skills and categorization skills
To increase ability to associate and combine information to reach a conclusion

Objectives

Receptive

The student will:

1. Sort items as magnetic and nonmagnetic

2. Classify items as iron and noniron

3. Conclude through association the relationship between magnets and iron

4. Comprehend the concept of change by using a magnet to make an iron object magnetic

5. Understand the difference between north and south as opposite directions

6. Comprehend the concept of *through* by discovering substances through which magnetic force can be conducted

Expressive

The student will:

1. Respond in a complete sentence, using a negative when appropriate

2. Verbally close sentences in a story-reading activity, using appropriate vocabulary

3. Express in sentences what happens when two magnets come together, using vocabulary words *repel/push away* and *attract/come together*

Vocabulary

magnetic	noniron	push away	north pole
horseshoe magnet	all	attract	south pole
bar magnet	some	repel	conduct
iron	come together	invisible	through

Lesson 1—*(Introductory)*
Magnets at Work

Objective—To sort objects according to whether or not they can be picked up by a magnet

Materials—

Horseshoe magnet
Items which will and will not be attracted to a magnet

Procedure—

1. Hold up the magnet and say, "This is a magnet." Have the children repeat the word *magnet*. "What is this? That's right, it is a magnet."

2. Spread the items that are and are not attracted to the magnet.

   a. Pick up some of the objects with the magnet. Ask, "What is this magnet doing?" *(Picking things up)*

   b. Try to pick up objects that not attracted to the magnet. Ask, "Is the magnet picking these things up?" *(No)*

   c. Ask: "Do magnets pick up *all* things? No, magnets pick up only *some* things."

3. "Let's sort our objects into two piles. In one pile we will put the things that the magnet picks up. In the other pile we will put the things that the magnet does not pick up."

   a. Select and name one object that will be attracted to the magnet. "This is a nail. Let's see if the magnet will pick up the nail."

   b. Test the object to show that it is picked up by the magnet.

   c. State the conclusion. "The nail was picked up by the magnet, so we'll put it here." Begin a pile.

   d. Select and name one object that will not be attracted to the magnet. "This is a crayon. Let's see if the magnet will pick up the crayon."

   e. Test the object to show that it is not picked up by the magnet.

   f. State the conclusion. "The crayon was not picked up by the magnet, so we'll put it here." Begin a second pile.

   g. Review the characteristic of each pile. "Remember, this pile is going to have objects that *are* picked up by the magnet. This pile is going to have objects that *are not* picked up by the magnet."

4. Give each child the magnet in turn. Ask the child:

   a. To select and name an object.

   b. To test the object.

   c. To state whether it was or was not picked up by the magnet.

   d. To place it on the appropriate pile.

Continue until all objects have been sorted.

Lesson 2—*(Introductory)*
Picking Up Iron

Objective—To show awareness that magnets pick up iron

Materials—

Horseshoe magnet
Items that are and are not attracted to magnets

Procedure—

1. Hold up the magnet, and ask, "What is this? Tell me all you can about this magnet." Help the children to recall the information learned in Lesson 1. Conclude. "A magnet can pick up some things; a magnet cannot pick up other things." Inform the children that a magnet is made of iron.

2. Name each item in the assortment of objects, and classify each. "This is a nail. It is made of iron ... This is a crayon. It is not made of iron." Separate the objects into iron and noniron piles as each object is considered.

3. Consider the pile of objects made of iron. Select one item and ask, "Is this made of iron?" Repeat for each item. Let the children pick up each object with the magnet.

   Review by pointing to the pile and asking, "How are all these things alike? What are these things made of? *(Iron)* Will a magnet pick them up?"

4. Consider the pile of noniron objects. For each item ask, "Is this made of iron?" Let the children try to pick up the objects with a magnet.

   Review by pointing to the pile and asking, "How are all these things alike? *(Not made of iron)* Will a magnet pick them up?"

5. Review that the magnet picks up only the things in the iron pile and not the things in the noniron pile. Try each object in the iron pile. Ask, "Did the magnet pick up the nail? Is the nail made of iron?" Try each object in the noniron pile. Ask, "Did the magnet pick up the crayon? Is the crayon made of iron?" Tell each child to use the magnet to pick up one thing made of iron.

Lesson 3—*(Reinforcement)*
Iron or Not Iron?

Objective—To use a magnet to identify iron and noniron objects

Materials—

Horseshoe magnets—one for each child
Iron and noniron items

Procedure—

1. Hold up an object made of iron. Show that the magnet picks it up. Ask, "Did the magnet pick up the nail? Is the nail made of iron? Yes, so we could say, The magnet picked up the nail because the nail is made of iron." Encourage the children to practice the sentence pattern by presenting several other objects made of iron and testing them.

2. Hold up a noniron object. Show that the magnet does not pick it up. Ask, "Did the magnet pick up the crayon? Is the crayon made of iron? No, so we could say, The magnet did not pick up the crayon because the crayon is not made of iron. Let's all say that. The magnet did not pick up the crayon because the crayon is not made of iron." Encourage the children to practice the sentence pattern by presenting and testing several other noniron objects.

3. Continue, using the above procedure to consider other iron and noniron objects. As the lesson progresses and the children gain practice with the sentence patterns, have them assume more responsibility for explaining what happens. Ask different children to watch and tell the others what happens and why (rather than merely "chorusing" the pattern sentence as a group).

4. Give each child a magnet. Instruct the children to walk around the room and locate objects that are or are not picked up by the magnet. Visit the children individually and ask them to explain their observations. Help the children to use the sentence patterns in their explanations.

Lesson 4—*(Reinforcement)* Magnet Story

Objective—To identify pictures of objects that a magnet will and will not pick up

Materials—

Copies of *Joseph's Magnet*
(See preparation instructions below)
Crayons—one for each child

Preparing the materials—Reproduce the story pages (pages 225-226). Make one copy for each child and one for a demonstration copy. Cut the pages apart along the dotted lines. Assemble the pages and staple them along the left margin to form books.

Procedure—

1. Review by asking children to recall information learned previously about magnets. *(They are made of iron, they pick up objects made of iron, they do not pick up noniron objects.)* Supply any ideas the children don't mention.

2. Using the demonstration copy of *Joseph's Magnet*, show the children the cover. Explain that the words on the cover tell the title of the story. They tell what the story is about. Read the title.

3. Give each child a copy of the book. "Who can tell me the title of this book? Now, open your book to the first page, and I'll read the words." If necessary, help the children find Page 1. Read the words and ask the children to provide the missing word.

   "Turn the page again." Read the words. Ask the children to put their fingers on the object the magnet would pick up.

   "Turn the page." Read the words. Have the children point to the two objects the magnet would not pick up.

4. Read the book again. This time have the children mark the appropriate pictures on each page.

Lesson 5—*(Extension)* Magnetizing

Objective—To magnetize objects

Materials—

Strong bar magnet—one for each child
50 nails, #10 or larger
50 steel welding rods
20 large wooden matches with the heads cut off
20 toothpicks
Straight pins

Procedure—

1. Show a bar magnet. Explain that it is a magnet and has the same capabilities as the horseshoe magnet. Demonstrate. Then say, "We've learned that magnets can pick up things that are made with iron. We've also learned that magnets are made of iron. Today we'll talk about how pieces of iron can be magnetized—how they can be made into magnets so they will be able to pick up other iron things."

2. Pick up a nail. "Is this a magnet?" Demonstrate that it is not a magnet by trying to pick up a straight pin with it. Then say, "The nail is not a magnet, but we can magnetize it—we can make it into a magnet—because it is made of iron. Watch." Stroke the nail with the bar magnet 30 or 40 times in one direction, lifting the magnet after each stroke. Count the strokes aloud, and encourage the children to count with you. Demonstrate that the nail is now magnetized by picking up a straight pin with it. "What did we do to the nail? Yes, we magnetized it. We were able to magnetize it because it is made of iron."

3. "Here is a match. Is the match made of iron? No, it's made of wood. Do you think we'll be able to magnetize the match? Let's try it." Stroke the match with the bar magnet 30 or 40 times in one direction, lifting the magnet after each stroke. Count the strokes aloud, and encourage the children to count with you. Attempt to pick up a straight pin with the match. "Were we able to magnetize the match? Why not?" *(It's not made of iron.)*

4. Hold up a toothpick, "Do you suppose we would be able to magnetize this? Why not?" Hold up a welding rod. "Do you suppose we would be able to magnetize this? Why?" Hold up a nail other than the one previously magnetized. "Do you suppose we would be able to magnetize this nail? Why?"

5. "Now each of you will magnetize something. Remember, the object has to be made of iron, and you'll also need a magnet." Give each child a bar magnet. Review once more how to magnetize an object by selecting a welding rod and demonstrating how it can be magnetized. As you demonstrate, verbalize the procedure. Be sure to emphasize that you must stroke in one direc-

tion, that the magnet must be lifted from the object after each stroke, and that the object must be stroked many times.

6. Spread the nails, rods, matches, and toothpicks on the table. Ask each child to select two objects that could be magnetized. Note their choices. If necessary, correct any errors. Then say, "Now you have an iron object and a magnet. Work by yourself and magnetize the iron object. I'll give each of you a pin, so you'll be able to see if you did make a magnet." The child's success on the task is demonstrated if the object will pick up a straight pin. After a reasonable time, help those children who failed to make a magnet from the nail or rod.

Lesson 6—(Extension) Magnetic Force

Objective—To state whether two bar magnets were attracted or repelled

Materials—Bar magnets—two for each child (See preparation instructions below)

Preparing the materials—Mark the north poles (N) of the magnets with paint or tape.

Procedure—

1. "We have learned that magnets hold on to iron things. It is a magnetic force that holds the iron things to a magnet. This magnetic force is invisible; we cannot see it."

Place two bar magnets close to each other with the N pole of one next to the S pole of the other. Ask the children to watch what happens. Explain that when the magnets come together, we say they are "attracted." Have them practice saying the word. Let each child bring the opposite poles of the two magnets in line in order to feel and see the two magnets come together.

Repeat, matching N to N. "Did the magnets come together? No, they pushed away. When they push apart, we say they are repelled." Let each child bring the similar poles together and feel and see the repelling action.

2. Give each child two magnets. Allow the children to experiment. Help each child to "feel" what the magnets do and to use the words *attract* and *repel*. Frequently repeat the association. "When the magnets come together, we say they are *attracted*; when they push apart, we say they are *repelled*."

3. Visit with each child in turn.

   a. Place the bar magnet poles N to N. Ask the child what happened.
   b. Place the bar magnet poles N to S. Ask the child what happened.
   c. Place the poles either N to N or N to S. Ask the child what happened.

Lesson 7—(Extension) Magnetic Conductors

Objective—To discover substances through which magnetic force can be conducted

Materials

Horseshoe or bar magnet
Cardboard
Metal dish or pan
Dish containing water
Thin piece of wood
20 to 30 straight pins

Procedure—

1. Place the pins on the table. Hold the magnet in the air. "Do you suppose this magnet will pick up the pins? Why?" *(The pins are made of iron, a magnet picks up iron objects.)* Ask a child to pick up the pins with the magnet.

2. Remove the pins from the magnet and place them on the table. Place a piece of paper on top of the pins. "If we leave the paper on top of the pins, do you suppose the magnet will be able to pick up the pins?" Ask another child to pick up the pins with the magnet.

3. "Remember yesterday" (Lesson 6), "we said we couldn't see magnetic force but we could see what it does? Remember how the magnets were sometimes attracted and sometimes repelled? Today we'll learn another new word to use when we talk about magnets. The word is *conducted.* Let's all say that. The magnet picks up the pins because the magnetic force is conducted—it goes through—the paper. The paper doesn't stop the magnetic force. The magnetic force is conducted through the paper."

4. "Let's see what other kinds of things conduct the magnetic force—what other kinds of things the force can go through." Have the children take turns testing the following situations:

    a. Place the pins under a piece of cardboard. Conclude. "Cardboard conducts the magnetic force."

    b. Place the pins in a dish of water. Conclude. "Water conducts the magnetic force."

    c. Place the pins under a metal dish. Conclude. "Metal conducts the magnetic force."

    d. Place the pins under a piece of thin wood. Conclude. "Wood conducts the magnetic force."

5. Place the pins on the table again. Hold the magnet above the pins. "What is between the magnet and the pins now? Is it cardboard? Is it water? Is it metal? Is it wood? No, but there is something that we can't see between the pins and the magnet. Who knows what it is?" *(Air)* "Watch and see if air conducts the magnetic force." Slowly bring the magnet closer to the pins. Point out to the children that you are not going to touch the pins with the magnet, but you will hold the magnet above the pins. When the magnet gets close enough to the pins, the pins will be attracted to it. After this has occurred, ask, "Does air conduct the magnetic force?"

In a follow-up lesson, show the children that although magnetism is conducted through many materials, whether the object can be picked up depends on the strength of the magnet and the thickness of the material. For instance, pins covered by a piece of paper may be picked up by a magnet, but pins covered by a ream of paper may not be picked up by the same magnet.

JOSEPH'S MAGNET

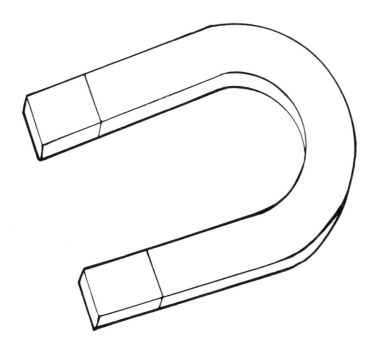

One day Joseph was walking on the sidewalk.

He looked down and saw a piece of paper.

Under the paper was a _____ .

1

Joseph picked up the magnet and went on walking.

He saw a nail and a stone on the sidewalk.

He knew that the magnet would pick up the _____ .

So he picked it up with his magnet.

2

When he got home, Joseph saw a paper clip
and a match
and a box on his father's desk.

He knew the magnet would not pick up the _____ .

He knew the magnet would not pick up the _____ .

So he didn't even try to pick them up.

He just picked up the _____ with his magnet.

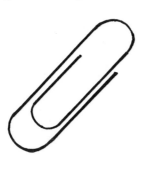  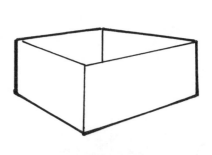

3

Help your young students explore their world with these activities . . .

EXCELL: Experiences in Context for Early Language Learning (1989)
by Catherine B. Raack, M.A., CCC-SLP

This field-tested resource features 70 topics to use in sensorimotor activities with your moderately to severely developmentally delayed, prelinguistic students. Students learn through theme based activities and active participation utilizing physical objects, pictures and songs of objects or events, and one-on-one group interaction. Resource includes guidelines, reproducible illustrations and a recordkeeping form to track your student's progress. **Catalog No. 7592-Y $19.95**

MONTH BY MONTH
Language Enrichment Activities for Early Learning (1988)
by Kay Barclay and Kathi Buche

New 12-month curriculum for your kindergarten and preschool students offers creative language activities for every month of the year. Each of these 12 units is based on a fun theme appropriate to the season—and all of the activities reinforce targeted vocabulary and teach basic skills such as math and following directions. **Catalog No. 7582 $49**

LET'S EXPERIMENT
Using Language in Science (1989)
by Carolyn Tavzel, M.S., CCC-SLP

Your students become active participants in these language lessons using science experiments. As students discuss the experiment, they can improve semantic and functional language skills, syntax and morphology, and problem-solving skills. You'll have experiments in air, colors, magnets, plants, sunshine, taste, temperature, and water. **Catalog No. 7612-Y $16.95**

ORDER FORM

Ship to: _____

_____

☐ Please check here if this is a permanent address change.
Please note previous zip code _____
Telephone (_____) _____ ☐ work ☐ home

Payment options:

☐ My personal check is enclosed. Please add 10% for shipping and handling.

☐ My school / clinic / hospital purchase order is enclosed.
P. O. # _____
Please add 10% for shipping and handling.

☐ Charge to my credit card. Please add 10% for shipping and handling.
☐ Visa ☐ MasterCard ☐ American Express

Card No. _____
Expiration Date: Month _____ Year _____
Signature _____

Qty.	Cat. #	Title	Amount
		Add 10% for shipping and handling. Arizona residents add sales tax.	
		TOTAL	

MONEY BACK GUARANTEE After purchasing, you'll have 90 days of risk-free evaluation. If you're not completely satisfied, return your order within 90 days for a full refund of the purchase price. NO QUESTIONS ASKED! Thank you for your order!
Send your order form to:

Communication Skill Builders
3830 E. Bellevue / P.O. Box 42050 –Y
Tucson, Arizona 85733